voices of diversity

voices of diversity

Real People Talk about Problems and Solutions in a Workplace Where Everyone Is Not Alike

Renee Blank   Sandra Slipp

American Management Association

New York • Atlanta • Boston • Chicago • Kansas City • San Francisco • Washington, D.C.
Brussels • Mexico City • Tokyo • Toronto

This book is available at a special
discount when ordered in bulk quantities.
For information, contact Special Sales Department,
AMACOM, a division of American Management Association,
135 West 50th Street, New York, NY 10020.

Library of Congress Cataloging-in-Publication Data

Blank, Renee.
    Voices of diversity / Renee Blank and Sandra Slipp.
       p. cm.
    Include bibliographical references and index.
    ISBN 0-8144-0217-8
    1. Minorities—Employment. 2. Multiculturalism. 3. Communication in personnel management. 4. Interpersonal relations. I. Slipp, Sandra. II. Title.
HF5549.5.M5B55   1994
331.6—dc20
                                       94-13517
                                         CIP

Printing number

10 9 8 7 6 5 4 3 2 1

Dedicated to our
parents
whose values guided us

and

To **Bob** and our loving family
R.B.

To **Sam** and **Elena**
S.S.

Contents

Preface and Acknowledgments

How did *Voices of Diversity* come to be? What made us take on the exhilarating but difficult task of interviewing hundreds of people, reviewing existing research and information on managing diversity, simplifying the complex issues of group and individual identity and stereotyping, and, finally, crafting a book that would provide understanding while being immediately practical?

Our impetus came from two directions: first, our academic backgrounds, and second, a professional need. We met as graduate students in New York University's Department of Human Relations and Social Policy in the late 1960s, a period of tremendous social turmoil—especially over the issue of race. Both of us were drawn to this department because it was one of the few places in the United States that focused on applied behavioral science—using the accumulated knowledge in the behavioral sciences to solve the social concerns of society. As graduate students, we designed field projects in organizations and read and researched widely in interdisciplinary areas: sociology, psychology, anthropology, and management. Our interests crystallized in management and organizational behavior, group dynamics, and social policy. We were trained to go out into the world, help create the emerging field of what was then called intergroup relations, and become change agents!

And we did just that. In the mid-1970s, we formed our own management and training consulting firm, Organizational, Planning and Training Associates, Inc. (OPT). Those were the years of class-action suits against large corporations for discrimination against women and minorities. We were initially involved in helping organizations deal with compliance issues under Title VII of the Civil Rights Act of 1964. Then, as many organizations dealt with basic compliance issues, we felt compelled to move beyond merely seeking formal compliance to analyzing subtle and difficult interpersonal issues and the complex systemic organization barriers that impede the full utilization of all employees.

Because there was very little practical information to use in diversity training, we designed our own materials. We wrote more than fifty training manuals for corporations and designed hundreds of role-play situations, case studies, and video scripts. During the next eighteen years, we honed our skills, listened, and learned as we trained thousands of managers and supervisors in working with a diverse workforce.

Along the way terminology changed. From intergroup and human relations specialists, we became diversity specialists. Instead of providing training primarily on issues of race, ethnicity, and gender, we broadened our range to include disability, sexual orientation, and age—all the subjects included in this book.

Hand-in-hand with our work on diversity issues, we were involved in management development training. We knew that it was essential to join diversity issues with basic issues of management and supervision: the two are inseparable. One of our earliest training pieces linked the relationship between equal employment opportunity (EEO) and key management issues: orientation, communication, performance appraisal, team building, training, and career development.

The second impetus for the book came from the continuing frustration felt both by us and by the training population. We consistently heard from hundreds of managers and supervisors that the literature on diversity was geared to legal compliance or concepts for the human resources professional but that there was no easily readable, practical, how-to book for managers or supervisors. And we kept hearing the urgent appeal from members of different groups that participated in our seminars who said, "No one understands what it's really like for us in the workplace. How do we get the word out?"

We knew there was a great need for a book that would offer immediate help with issues of diversity. We had heard so much from managers and workers, and we had already written extensively on this topic.

As we put our material together and assessed the needs in the workplace, we determined that the book would not be a book primarily on EEO compliance; it would not be a book on systemic organizational development; it would not be a book on the culture, history, or anthropology of each major group. These books had been written and are important. We touch on these topics throughout our book. But the book that needed to be written would offer an answer to the urgent managerial appeal: "What should I know about the experience of the diverse groups?" and "What should I do about it?"

We are indebted to many. Professor Dan Dodson, who headed the New York University Department of Human Relations and Social Policy, inspired us greatly. He was an academic, a practitioner, a pragmatist, and an idealist—a believer in the possibility of change. Another key person is Dr. Kenneth B. Clark, the noted psychologist, whom we first met through his writings. We were fortunate that he was one of our first training colleagues and continues as a mentor and friend. From each of our clients—the training directors, human resource professionals, and the participants—we continue to learn.

Each chapter in this book was read by specialists in and advocates for the particular group discussed. We especially want to thank Lorraine Cortez-Vasquez, Chris Almvig, Morton Fromer, Laura Huber, Dr. Josie Smith, Valerie-Oliver Durrah, Dr. Hae Ahm Kim, Dr. Nicholas Montaldo, Janet Chu, Dr. Setsuko Nishi, Judy Roberts Seto, Dr. Mario Rendon, and Robert Webber for their invaluable comments and suggestions.

We owe much to our husbands, authors themselves, Dr. Samuel Slipp and Dr. Robert Blank, for their ongoing encouragement and advice. Also of great help was Dr. Paula Blank and especially Paul Aron, who offered early encouragement on the book's importance and publishability and continuous advice and assistance on style and content. We also thank our agent, Edward Knappman, for his good counsel and our editor, Adrienne Hickey, for her insights and support.

Above all, we owe thanks to the "voices" of the interviewees and workshop participants, for their enthusiasm and their willingness to tell us their stories, with specific workplace examples. There was an urgency, almost a plea, from members of every group—the receptionist who is disabled, the gay computer programmer, the twenty-two-year-old management trainee, the sixty-year-old, white, male engineer, the pregnant marketing analyst, the refugee working in the garment industry, the African-American stockbroker, the Asian-American chemist, the Latino social service director. *They all wanted managers to know about them.* Long after we completed the manuscript, our phones rang as workers from every group called us to tell their story. So this is *their* story, their book, and to them—the voices from the diverse workforce—we are deeply grateful.

Part One
The Changing Workplace

Chapter 1
Introduction

Diversity and *multiculturalism* are two of the newest and hottest words for the workplace of the 1990s. And no wonder! Here are a few of the dramatic facts about the changing workforce:

- Women, people of color, and immigrants (many non-English speaking) represent more than 50 percent of the present workforce.
- By 2000, 85 percent of the *entering* workforce will be female, African-American, Asian-American, Latino, or new immigrants.
- Two million "older" workers, between ages 50 and 64, are ready, willing, and able to work and are not being utilized. Within twenty-five years, one out of every four workers will be age 55 or older.
- Of the 43 million people with disabilities in this country, many will seek equal opportunity in employment, encouraged by the Americans with Disabilities Act of 1990.

The impact of these startling demographics is already being felt in the workplace. Diverse groups bring different expectations in work styles, needs, and values, and managers must learn to make diversity an asset to improve working relationships and productivity.

Much of the writing on diversity, especially in the workplace, offers generalizations *about* what to do or how to react in certain situations. For example, you're told, "Try to be more sensitive to differences." But that is a far cry from knowing exactly what you may be saying or doing that offends others or is insensitive to their feelings and values.

This book describes, in the words of the members of each group, what actually offends them and what they resent about their treatment in the workplace. These offenses can be either (1) blatant stereotyping or (2) insensitivities, subtle or not-so-subtle, to cultural needs or differences. The book describes real situations experienced by women, Latinos, Asian-Americans, African-Americans, white men, young workers, older workers, people with disabilities, and gays and lesbians. The material was gathered through hundreds of interviews and eighteen years of conducting workshops on managing a diverse workplace for private corporations, government agencies, and educational institutions.

An important premise of this book is that many people are uncomfortable dealing with people who are different from themselves and don't realize when they are being insensitive to others. Also, many people feel uncomfortable even discussing or admitting that there are any differences among people. They feel that a discussion of differences reinforces stereotypes, most of which are negative. We disagree. People do stereotype, and stereotypes already exist that have detrimental effects on group members' treatment in the workplace. Misunderstandings, misjudgments, and managerial mistakes often stem from a lack of awareness of the *reactions* of group members to insensitive remarks and behaviors and prejudgments about capabilities.

The book is written from the perspectives of and through the voices of group members who feel that it is extremely important that their experiences and perspectives be known, because these can have a direct impact on how they are viewed and treated in the workplace.

A major theme of this book is that many people may unintentionally or subconsciously behave in a way that has a negative effect on others. We know that racism, sexism, and all kinds of other isms exist and that bigotry and prejudice are facts of life. But we also believe that many people want to be open-minded but are simply not aware of the effect of their words and behavior on others.

This is a how-to book for all workers, but especially for supervisors and managers. It explains how to cope with the most typical and difficult interactions that occur within a diverse workforce. After describing the perspectives of each group, we will present workplace examples and a model of what supervisors and managers can do and say as they deal with different values, styles of work, communication and language problems, and motivational issues.

Managers and supervisors need information about the perspectives of different groups in the workplace. If such information helps managers recognize and use positive traits in people different from themselves, this book will help make better managers. And if our illustrations of stereotyping help managers realize that they've assumed something about a person that just isn't true, this book will have made not only better managers but people better equipped to live in an increasingly diverse society.

Chapter 2

Group Identity,
Group Tendencies,
Individual Differences,
and Stereotypes

There is an inherent conflict in considering workforce diversity because of the need to see each worker both as an individual and as a member of a group.

On the one hand, the bottom-line advice to managers is to view each worker as an individual, to evaluate his or her individual strengths, skills, and promotability, and not to categorize or stereotype the worker on the basis of group membership. Each person, regardless of group membership, is innately different and has had unique life experiences and so will not be exactly like other members of that group. People interviewed for the book, in all groups, repeatedly said, "Tell your readers we are not all the same."

On the other hand, the manager should be aware that an individual worker's behavior and perspective may be affected, influenced, or enhanced by that worker's membership in a particular group, that is, his or her *group identity*.

Thus, the people interviewed who said "we are not all the same" also said "members of our group do share some common characteristics or experiences, and we want our background and experiences known to others, particularly as they affect our situation in the workplace."

Are these two concepts—individual uniqueness and group

identity—contradictory? Not at all. A key to supervising an individual worker effectively is knowing as much as possible about that worker. Group identity is simply another factor—and often an important one—in helping a manager understand an individual employee's behavior and perspective.

Effective supervisors or managers have always been aware of personality, educational background, and past work experience as variables influencing individual behavior. But race, ethnicity, age, gender, sexual orientation, or disability have not been properly recognized as important factors in explaining behavior. When group identity is recognized, it is often in terms of stereotypes—categorizing individuals *only* by their group identity—rather than seeing group identity as one part of a complex individual. Such stereotyping is often characterized by blatantly negative or mistaken interpretations of a group tendency.

Group Identity and Group Tendencies

Members of groups share some similar values, beliefs, behavior, background, and/or experiences. These are defined as the group's *culture*. In this book we sometimes use the term *group tendencies*, instead of culture, because culture is often used to describe ethnic or nationality groups. The meaning of the term *culture* has in recent years also been expanded to describe other groups (the culture of the deaf or gay culture). The groups described in this book are varied; some are based on ethnicity and nationality, others on race, gender, sexual orientation, age, or disability.

Cultural and group tendencies are dynamic and change over time. They are not the same for all members of the group. Nevertheless, cultural or group tendencies, although fluid, exist. Women tend to have a more participatory, interactive management style than men. Latinos tend not to separate work and personal relationships as much as most non-Latinos do.

Members of each of the groups described in this book share some common values, experiences, attitudes, and perspectives, and these often influence their behavior. If someone shares these tendencies, they are part of that person's *group identity*.

Most important, group members share the experience of

being viewed in terms of the stereotypes that others have about them.

Individual Differences and Group Identity

How then does one account for individual differences between group members? Psychologists and sociologists agree that group identity, only one part of individual identity, varies for each individual by many factors not addressed in this book, such as personality, social class, geographic location, occupation, and life experiences. Thus, it is often said that there are more differences within groups than between groups. For example, a group tendency for Asian-Americans may be politeness, but if a person has a "hot temper," this will override the cultural norm of politeness.

People born into a group also vary on how strongly they choose to identify with the group. For some, group membership may be the most salient part of their identity. For others, it is not. Some choose not to identify with the group at all and disavow most or all of the group tendencies as much as possible, at least on a conscious level. Yet even these people find that part of their group identity affects their perspective.

For virtually all immigrant groups or individuals, a process of acculturation takes place along a continuum ranging from total identification with one's original culture to the assimilation of some or all of the new culture. For many, there is an attempt to hold onto a proud cultural heritage and at the same time become a mainstream American. The choice is seen not as either/or but as both. Identification with two cultures often continues through many generations.

Stereotyping

Stereotyping attributes to all individuals in a group the characteristics or tendencies of some. Moreover, the stereotype usually exaggerates a group tendency and is usually negative or has a negative impact.

Stereotypes are often popularly held beliefs perpetuated by

the media and unchallenged in people's minds because they have not had any personal experience to counteract the stereotypes. Those who belie the stereotype are seen as exceptions.

Stereotypes serve a function, often subconscious. If you can put a label on someone, you can feel justified in practicing certain behaviors. If you think Asian-Americans are good only in technical areas, you can restrict them to perform only in these areas. If you think women cannot gain credibility with top customers, you don't have to promote them to senior positions. If you think people with disabilities have poor attendance records, you don't have to hire them. Thus, the effect of stereotyping, whether intentional or not, is to subordinate the group.

Differences between Stereotypes and Group Tendencies

The following are blatant stereotypes:

- People with disabilities cannot work regular hours.
- Women who are mothers aren't committed to their jobs.
- White men are racists and sexists.
- Immigrants do not want to learn English.

In these cases the characteristics of some members of a given group are attributed to all members of the group. Yes, these characteristics are true for some members of the groups but not for most, and certainly not for all.

What, then, is the difference between a stereotype and a group tendency? As we have said, some characteristics or group tendencies do exist for many members—although not all members—of a group. In the case of racial and ethnic groups, we commonly refer to these as cultural differences.

Sometimes there is a fine line between a group characteristic and a stereotype. For example, many immigrants come from non-English-speaking countries and many—not all—have trouble speaking English after they arrive and prefer to speak their own language on the job if possible. Thus, a group tendency is that many immigrants have difficulty speaking English after they arrive in the United States. This tendency then causes a stereotype to arise, namely, that all immigrants do not want to or are unable to learn English. Another example: Many people with disabilities—although not all—may need some accommodation so that they can perform their job. A stereotype is that people with disabilities cannot work because it is too hard for them and their employers.

What is harmful about stereotypes is that they don't allow people to be seen as individuals with unique skills, strengths, and, yes, group characteristics—in some cases.

A stereotype is invariably negative or has a negative effect on the person stereotyped, whereas a description of a group tendency helps in understanding the perspectives of the group member.

Aren't People Members of Many Groups?

Yes, everyone is a member of many groups. The work experience of an older Asian-American woman with a disability who is a lesbian would be partially described in five of the chapters in this book, or six if she is a recent immigrant. Only baby-boomer, white, non-Latino, heterosexual, nondisabled men and women will find themselves described in only one of the chapters. And they, too, have multiple group identities growing out of ethnic, religious, regional, professional, or other group memberships not described in this book.

For people with membership in several groups, different aspects of their group identity may be more important at a given time.

The book is arranged by groups to highlight the special issues each of the groups faces, despite the fact that many people may find themselves in more than one category.

Summary

A critical tenet of this book is that people, both coworkers and managers, too often go to one extreme or the other regarding group members. Either they attribute only the group identity to a member, which generally means seeing a particular worker in a stereotypical way, or they totally ignore or fail to appreciate a group characteristic or tendency that may influence someone's behavior and perspective.

A good example of this is the impassioned statement by a worker with a spinal injury that requires her to use a wheelchair.

> I am not a wheelchair. Yet some people treat me as if that is the only important factor about me and somehow define me as a "defective person." I am a skilled accountant, with ten years of experience; I am a wife and a mother. I come from the South. I love music. My friends and family tell me I have a good sense of humor. All of these describe who I am. On the other hand, as it is for virtually everyone who must use a wheelchair, accessibility is an important issue for me, yet people often totally ignore this factor when planning a meeting or selecting my work-site. And then they wonder why it is difficult for me to do my work. It seems as if people either think of me only as a person in a wheelchair or totally ignore the fact that I do have special needs.

The goal of the book is to help managers appreciate workers as individuals, as well as members of a group.

A caveat: This book is not intended to be a definitive study of every group discussed. Instead, it illustrates some important tendencies in each group and the experiences of these workers that may affect personal interaction, teamwork, and promotional opportunities in the workplace.

For many group members, none of the issues discussed in the book may apply. But this book is written about those group members who *have* experienced these problems and for managers who are willing to listen to the voices in the diverse workforce so that they can truly maximize the value of every individual worker.

Part Two
The Diverse Voices

Chapter 3

African-Americans

The terms *African-American* and *black* are used interchangeably in this chapter because both are widely accepted. The increasing popularity of the term *African-American* attests to the strengthened cultural awareness of people who trace their heritage and identity to Africa, particularly sub-Saharan Africa. Included in those considered African-American are immigrants from the West Indies, although they do not view their culture and experience as similar to those of American-born blacks.

There is a wide range of diversity within the black community, including differences in place of birth within the United States, social class, and education.

African-Americans currently make up 12.1 percent of the population, almost 30 million people.[1] At present, they are the largest minority group in the United States and in the workforce. Although a disproportionate number are represented among the lowest-income workers, 36 percent of black households in 1990 were classified as middle-class, i.e., earning more than $25,000, and of this group, 11.5 percent earned more than $50,000 a year.

The growth of the black middle class is a relatively new phenomenon. In the late 1960s, barely 5 percent of blacks were considered middle-class and another 5 percent upper-middle-class.[2]

The large increase in African-American participation in the middle class was fueled by the 1960s civil rights movement, which led to equal employment opportunity laws, affirmative action programs, and minority set-asides, all of which helped blacks gain access to white-collar employment.

What distinguishes African-Americans most from other groups is their visibility of color and the dominant white culture's negative perception of them as a group, compared to other groups. Although some nonwhite Asian and Latino immigrant groups have in time crossed the line and earned reluctant acceptance by whites, the barrier of color is much harder for blacks to surmount. Despite their increasing number in positions of power in the workplace, most blacks fully understand and expect that they will encounter obstacles and inequities.

Despite the enormous diversity among African-Americans, sociologists have attributed several cultural tendencies to this group: directness and spontaneity, expressiveness, sense of community, and a great regard for family and religion. Although there may be disagreement by some cultural specialists regarding these attributes, none would disagree about the debilitating effects of racism or about the remarkable fact that many blacks, despite incredible odds, have had the emotional and physical strength to survive and succeed in the workplace.

Voices of African-Americans in the Workplace

Many African-American workers say they can never get away from color as an identifier; they are always seen as blacks, not as just human beings.

A senior executive said, "You are always the *black* person—the black accountant, the black lawyer. Race is always our identifier—our badge. And the definition of what black means is imposed by the dominant white culture, which sees black as inferior."

When a highly acclaimed scholar who has written extensively about blacks in the United States was asked what he thought was most important for whites to know about blacks in the workplace, he sighed wearily and said, with tremendous sadness, "Just say that we're human beings."

Many African-American workers say that they are rarely given personal credit for their achievements.

An insurance analyst said, "People always seem to make an excuse for our achievement. It is assumed that we gained our position solely because of an EEO or affirmative action initiative and not because of our ability or experience; once on the job, if we do well, people assume that our white colleagues helped us out or even did our work! Finally, if they do recognize our ability, it's assumed that we are an 'exception.' "

A university administrator said, "Despite the number of articles I've published in major academic journals, my extensive administrative work on committees, and my reputation as one of the best teachers on campus, I always have the feeling that others think I got something I didn't quite deserve. *The simple fact of being intelligent and working hard to achieve something doesn't seem to be allowed to us.* People always seem to feel that we got something we didn't deserve, that excuses, favors, or exceptions of judgment are made for us—I'm made to feel that I can never really 'own' my success."

The irony of these statements is that most blacks interviewed say that they have to work twice as hard and be twice as good as whites in order to be considered competent and reliable.

Many African-American workers say that others do not believe them when they describe discrimination.

A budget analyst told his white peer that a secretary assumed he was a messenger when he went to another floor to present a report to a senior executive. "You're Donald Grey from the finance department?" the secretary said in disbelief. When told this, the white peer chided the black worker for feeling offended and implied this could happen to anyone. "You're too sensitive," he said.

A loan officer was told by his supervisor that a client said that he didn't want to work with "that kind"—referring to the black loan officer. In telling the loan officer about the incident, the white supervisor said she assumed this was just an isolated instance. When the loan officer said that this kind of discrimination and racism happen all the time in both obvious and subtle ways, the white supervisor said, "Don't overreact. *I've* never seen this happen before."

Many African-American workers say that there is often a "code of silence" for both blacks and whites when it comes to discussing race.

"We have learned not to talk much about race," a black attorney said. "There is a conspiracy of silence that is agreed upon by both races. If blacks complain, they look like victims, and no one wants to be seen as a victim. If you're successful and you talk about discrimination, whites say, 'Why are you complaining—you have it made.' And mostly, we don't talk about race because whites are very uncomfortable about the subject. They think that talking about racism means an indictment of all whites, including themselves. So both groups perpetuate a facade of amiability and denial."

A secretary in a consumer products company said, "The only time race comes up is if there is a riot someplace and then I'm supposed to be the big expert. I feel as if I'm somehow blamed for all the trouble. Believe it or not, people ask me, 'Why are you people still so mad?' I really don't know what to say or where to begin, so I just shrug and keep my mouth shut."

Many African-American workers say they do not receive standard amounts of feedback on their work; they receive either too much or too little.

"We feel we are oversupervised; every letter sent out is scrutinized," said a trainee in a brokerage house. Others say they get little or no feedback because supervisors seem to feel that if they give any criticism, black workers will assume they are racists.

A black equipment salesman, newly hired, said, "I hear white workers getting specific, constructive—and very helpful—feedback on how they can improve their relationships with customers. The feedback many blacks get is somehow 'off'—and not really helpful. Either someone wants to act like a nice guy or my friend and will give me some phony stroking—'Great job!'—for something very ordinary, or they will exaggerate a mistake I made and make a really big deal out of it. I always get the feeling that I'm not really learning anything from the feedback I get."

Many African-American workers say that they constantly have to prove themselves to each new person they meet; their past achievements do not "travel" with them.

A black fiscal officer said, "Your reputation for excellence doesn't follow you. For everyone who's new, you have to prove yourself—and constantly. It's a continuing process. The first thing that's seen is your blackness, which is associated with a lack of ability and competence. It's assumed that you won't have the right answer. Maybe that's why people don't seem to really listen when we speak."

"And even after you *are* known, you can never relax," said a consumer affairs manager in a large food company, who added that he notices that white colleagues on his level seem to be able to relax once they've made it. "We are always being tested."

Over and over, blacks say that it is just assumed that a white is competent until proven incompetent. The reverse is true for blacks. "It is assumed that we are incompetent or somehow flawed, until we prove over a long haul that we're not," said a black compensation specialist.

A black clerk in a bank said, "It amazes me that even if a white is dumb, he'll be trusted more than a black to do a job." A black firefighter said, "We are not seen as smart as whites, and it is assumed that our character—honesty and reliability—is not as good."

Many African-Americans say they are resented when they excel.

A black hospital administrator said, "Whites simply have a hard time if they are not in a superior position to blacks; it is such a part of our culture. Most whites don't think they can learn anything from blacks about achievement. Not only are whites continually surprised when we come up with good ideas, they find it difficult to accept a solution that is not suggested by someone white. People seem to actually resent my successes."

A black industrial psychologist explained, "It's like cognitive dissonance—holding two contrary ideas at the same time. It's a good idea, but it came from a black person. To some whites this seems like a contradiction, as well as an affront to their superiority."

Some blacks say that they think whites are definitely more comfortable if blacks are passive and *not* achievers.

Many African-Americans say that the few abuses of affirmative action, i.e., when an unqualified person got a position, are not seen as an exception but are believed to be the norm.

A black director of EEO and affirmative action explained, "Weren't whites ever hired who weren't competent? Are there any mediocre whites? You'd think the only incompetents are blacks who were hired as part of affirmative action plans. Yes, there are incompetent blacks—just like incompetent whites." Also, this manager, as well as many others, feels that most of the "abuses" of affirmative action happened in the early years of EEO and affirmative action implementation, when companies would sometimes hire minorities quickly and without adequate screening simply in order to appear to be meeting legal requirements. "They were setting people up for failure," one personnel specialist remembered. "Sometimes, there really was not much of an attempt to find someone qualified. This backfired and gave affirmative action a bad reputation. Maybe it's a reaction to some of the mistakes of the early days, but it seems as if now every black has to be superqualified to be considered, and then others think we got the job only because of affirmative action."

Many blacks interviewed feel that affirmative action requirements did—and still do—play an important role in ensuring that blacks are at least considered for positions for which they are eligible.

Many African-Americans say they are tracked in support services— personnel, human resources, community relations—or into "black products" departments.

"There are certain places where it's comfortable to put us, but I feel it's a new kind of ghetto. It's hard to get into a supervisory line management position, and when we do, we generally have small budgets and few people report to us," said a community affairs associate. This respondent also said, as have many others, that blacks are usually not considered for top decision-making positions, particularly in the financial area.

A black college graduate who majored in marketing said that his best offers came from the "black products" divisions of several cosmetics companies. "There was just no comparison between the offers I got and the broad range offered to my classmates. Sure, I know I'm good in 'black marketing,' but I'd like to think that's not the only place I can function."

Many African-Americans say they are stuck in one job or department so that their boss can meet his or her EEO goals.

"Our bosses get credit on their evaluation for the recruitment and retention of black employees, but this is to our detriment. Our supervisors don't want to bother recruiting others, so they keep us in their department instead of recommending or developing us for promotion." This black sales representative added, "It's almost as if one white manager says to another, 'I've got mine; get your own black.'" A colleague concurred, saying, "This is just part of the same old pattern of assuming that there's a very limited quantity of qualified blacks; if they lose me, they think they can't get another black."

Many African-Americans say that others feel that being supervised by a black gives them lower status in the organization.

A black engineering unit head said, "It's assumed that we won't get as many resources, that we won't have the clout in the organization for new projects. And then again, there's the old thing about the black person's credibility. Is this person really capable of being a leader?"

Many black managers complain about subordinates who go over their heads because the employees assume that the black managers don't have authority or power and that their decisions aren't valid and need to be checked out. Even in meetings, blacks say they don't get the respect that a white manager would get from subordinates. This is carried further in management meetings with peers. A marketing manager said, "My suggestions are usually ignored and passed over. I feel like I'm like the guy in Ralph Ellison's book, *The Invisible Man*. I know I don't get the status a white gets in the same position."

Many African-Americans say that if they complain about anything, they are considered troublemakers or are assumed to have a "chip on their shoulders."

Many black workers say that if they have any grievance or complaint, it is not taken seriously. A layout artist at a newspaper said, "It's assumed that we're exaggerating or that we're looking for trouble. This is before we're even heard out."

Many African-Americans say that if they socialize with other blacks at lunch, they are seen as "planning something" or as segregating themselves.

A mailroom clerk said, "When we sit together at lunch, people think we're planning something. Whites get scared or annoyed when we stay together. But when the whites sit together, no one seems to think anything about it."

Many black workers say they like to socialize with other black colleagues, to swap "war stories," problem-solve, learn to cope, or just relax. A systems analyst said, "When I'm with other blacks, I feel as if I don't have to be 'on'—being scrutinized every minute, watching the way I talk or laugh. If we say something tasteless with whites, it's not forgiven—we've 'lost it.' "

Many African-Americans say that others don't realize the tremendous stress they continually experience for feeling that they are representing all blacks.

An assistant vice president in the corporate office of a bank said, "I am constantly on display. Every minute, I have to show that I am competent, honest, cooperative, pleasant. None of this is taken for granted. If I am irritable, it means I'm difficult to work with; if I complain, I'm uppity. If I laugh too loud or tell jokes, it means I'm unrefined and not serious about work. The pressure is enormous. Nothing we do is seen as an individual trait; it's always related to being black. I feel as if I am made to represent all black people."

Many African-Americans say that others don't understand their rage from the daily psychological assaults they endure because of race.

A marketing executive listed some of his experiences in a single week: "I can't get a cab. When I'm with a white colleague, he stands out in front; it's assumed I'm the chauffeur when I'm met by executives who don't know me; peers show surprise that I wrote an outstanding report; a racist joke is told and I'm considered humorless if I don't laugh; I'm taken for a shoplifter when I'm browsing in the record store during lunchtime; I'm seated in the back of a virtually empty restaurant when I take a client out to lunch.

"These daily 'assaults' can make me a little crazy and exhausted. Because I'm so used to racism, I sometimes don't know whether someone's reaction to me is due to racism, something that really is my fault, a personality quirk on the other person's part that doesn't have anything to do with me at all, or the normal way things are done in the organization. I get so tired of it all." A black training manager said, "Yes, most blacks are somewhat paranoid—we would have to be crazy if we weren't. The big issue is how to handle racism, blatant or subtle, when we see it. Most successful blacks have learned how to 'manage' racism, pick and choose the issues, try to get beyond it, and, mostly, not let it deter them from their own goals."

Many African-Americans say they are rarely part of the normal socializing in an organization.

A black engineer at a computer company said, "I feel really left out when I'm not invited to informal socializing, especially when it's during the workday. I know this is where informal contacts are made and information exchanged."

"Being part of the social loop is essential for my career, but blacks are never invited to a peer's or a superior's home for a purely social occasion—that's a given. Any sociability there is ends in the office," said a project manager at a large manufacturing company. "When we are invited to a required corporate occasion, many of us—and our spouses or significant others—feel uncomfortable. We feel as if we are being looked over; our every movement is scrutinized to see if we know how to act right—or 'white' enough."

Many African-Americans say their upward path to senior management is blocked because they have no mentors.

Many black managers report that they have few black role models in top management to emulate and that few whites will openly "sponsor" or mentor them. The natural process by which someone selects a manager to move up is often denied to blacks, who claim that they have to initiate the process to find a sponsor who will help them learn managerial skills and master the norms of the corporation and the political strategies needed for getting ahead. "For the most part, we are alone," said a senior corporate attorney.

Even when whites do want to serve as mentors, there are sometimes problems. A black male manager reported that his supervisor, a white woman, tried to support him and act as a mentor. He felt that they were looked upon with suspicion, as if the relationship had sexual overtones. "We became uncomfortable with this close business relationship, and we mutually agreed to distance ourselves from each other. I think she unintentionally put me in jeopardy," he said. Other blacks report that when whites mentor blacks, they sometimes act condescending and overly protective or expect blacks to be forever indebted to them.

An account executive said, "One of the partners in my firm seems to really want to help me, but he's killing me with kindness. He acts really protective and says things like 'I won't let you take this job until you're really prepared for it. I want to make sure you can really succeed so that you're not set up for failure. You need more experience.' But I already have more experience than others who've gotten opportunities here."

Many African-Americans say that the need to conform to white norms of management style saps them of their identity.

Most organizations reward conformity. To be "like whites" in the corporate world, however, many black employees and managers say that they have to repress their own identities. "Many of us are more spontaneous and expressive than some of our white counterparts, especially if we've grown up in a mostly segregated northern city," said one black manager. "We're not afraid of verbal conflict. We like to debate openly and to challenge ideas. But if we have an animated argument on an issue, we are seen as hostile or aggressive or as having an 'attitude.' It's as if everyone is comfortable with us only when we are passive. This is a problem, especially for young black workers."

A black receptionist said, "I always think about my speech—whether it sounds 'white enough.' And many of my friends try to act cool to show others that we are strong despite how we may be treated because we're black."

A fiscal officer in a governmental agency said, "We're in a box. When my white manager loses his temper and curses, that's considered acceptable behavior. If I did the same thing, I would be perceived as unstable, aggressive, and even potentially violent."

Many black workers report that an individualistic style of dressing is important to them. A black accounts manager in the health care industry said, "It proclaims our pride in our image and identity. Maybe it's because we are lumped together as one mass by society as 'black.' But in some places, you just won't get ahead unless you wear the corporate uniform."

Many African-American workers say that they are not allowed to take risks on the job.

"My boss seems to feel that it will reflect on him if I fail, so he prevents me from doing something really innovative and creative. And I've seen other blacks not get promoted because their bosses didn't want to take a chance on them," a product engineer reported. "We have to be given the opportunity to fail, just as whites fail. Occasionally we are allowed to take a risk, but our risk is twice as much as it is for someone who is white. If a white person fails, he fails as an individual. If I fail, I fail for myself, for my boss, and, of course, for all black people. But if we don't take risks, we'll never get ahead, and we need help from our white bosses to allow us the chance."

Many African-Americans say that whites think they don't know how to act right in the "white world," partly because whites' images of blacks come from the media.

A black management consultant said, "Many whites don't understand that most blacks are bicultural—they grow up learning how to act in both the white world and the black world. Many middle-class whites have grown up not knowing blacks of equal status and don't understand that middle-class blacks have the same values they do. It seems as if most whites don't have any idea of the vast black middle-class world—lawyers, doctors, accountants, teachers, writers, social workers. There are literally millions of black college graduates in the United States today, yet whites are always surprised at us."

A black accountant said, "I can't tell you how many times people have said to me, 'You don't act black.' When I ask what does 'acting black' mean, the answer always reflects the ghetto images in the media or criminals, sports figures, musicians, rappers. Yes, they're part of the black community, but it's not the whole part. It's amazing how little whites know about the range of black people."

Scenes from the Workplace

Style and Credibility

John Williams* is a black senior sales trainer for a large computer manufacturing company, a job he has held for six months. He had an outstanding record in sales and as a sales trainer and was asked to head up a new regional training unit to get it off and running. John has great enthusiasm and a reputation as a real go-getter. His style in training is assertive and challenging. His feedback is "direct and honest," as he himself would say. In fact, John takes pride in "telling it like it is." When asked about his style, he says, "Anyone in sales has to be tough. I know my people can take it. They better get used to the rough world out there."

Although most of the trainees regard John highly and see him as a role model because of his acknowledged reputation as a top salesman and trainer, several of the trainees have objected to the way that John has challenged them in class. They think he is too rough and confrontational in the way he gives feedback. Although John has offered to speak after class to anyone who wants additional assistance, several of the unhappy trainees don't speak to him about their concerns but instead go to John's boss, the director of sales, to complain. They say that John is "too aggressive and angry."

Pete Warren, the director of sales, is new to the job. Although he had heard some good things about John before coming to the department, he really didn't know that much about John's outstanding reputation. Moreover, he had never worked with a black manager as senior as John.

Pete calls John in and tells him that he is antagonizing some

*All workplace scenarios in this book are based on the experiences of several people. The names are fictional.

of the trainees and that he should "tone it down." "I don't know about how you worked with the previous director, but it seems to me that your style is too strong from what I'm hearing. I don't want to hear any more complaints from the sales reps. I hope you'll be able to work it out and do it the way I like things done here."

John thinks, "Here we go again. I have to prove myself all over again. I know if I were white, my style would be seen as an asset, especially in sales. What's seen as angry in me is seen as strong in a white guy."

What Went Wrong?

1. The new director of sales didn't seem to know about John's great reputation as a salesman and sales trainer or how successful his training style had been.
2. He took the complaints from a few trainees as "gospel," without checking whether these complaints were widespread.
3. He didn't encourage the trainees to discuss their complaints with John before discussing them with him, thereby undercutting John's authority.
4. He didn't hear John's side of the story.

What Should Have Been Done?

1. The director of sales should have known about John's past record, which was outstanding on sales performance and sales training.
2. He should have observed John himself and checked his own assumptions and those of the trainees about the effectiveness of John's style. Since sales is always a tough business, would there have been the same negative reactions to John's style if he were white?
3. He should have checked the background and experience of the trainees who were complaining.
4. He could have given John some feedback on how he might explain his style to those not used to his manner; that wouldn't mean that John would have to change but he

could at least learn to help the trainees understand that he is not, in fact, attacking them. He might have helped John to show the trainees the benefits of his assertive and forceful feedback style.

5. The director should have expressed strong support for John, told the trainees to raise their complaints with John directly, and suggested that the employees stretch their expectations of how people give feedback. If, after meeting with John directly, the employees still had problems with John's style, the director would then arrange a meeting with the trainees and John.

6. The director should meet with John periodically to assess the training and offer to work with him on areas that may be perceived as problematic.

What the Director of Sales Might Have Said

"John, I've heard great things about your record as a salesman and sales trainer and I'm pleased that you're in charge of the special training unit. I want to talk to you, though, about two of the trainees who have complained about your feedback style, which they seem to think is too tough. I haven't seen you in action, so I'm especially interested in hearing your side of the issue. I did, of course, tell them to raise their concerns directly with you."

If John explains that his style is direct, to the point, and forceful, the director might say, "Your rationale sounds fine, but you might want to explain to the group that your style is not meant to be an attack, even though it might seem more confrontational and direct than they are used to. I'm sure you can work it out with the group. I'm available to brainstorm with you on how to deal with any problem trainees you may have. I've been in this business a long time, and I'll be glad to share my experience with you. The new sales training unit is a high priority, and I want to help you in any way I can to make it really successful."

Isolation and Lack of Support

Fred La Monte, a black senior engineer, was recently hired as a manager to supervise twenty engineers. He had formerly held a similar job in a much smaller company. Although there are several other blacks in the organization, he is the highest ranking black manager.

Fred feels very confident about his expertise in the field, and he welcomes this opportunity to build on his past experience and to advance his career.

Four months into the job, Fred feels uneasy. When he first came, everyone seemed very cordial, but now he realizes that he is being excluded from information channels and informal meetings. He sees other people going out together for lunch and chatting during the day. But none of his coworkers have reached out to him, either to join them for lunch, meet after work for a drink, or even chat informally as they come into the office. A few times when he tried to join in conversations with his colleagues who were talking informally, he felt they were ill at ease, and there seemed to be an awkward silence as he approached.

He is determined to focus on the job itself. The procedures are somewhat different from those at his last job, and the software is vastly different. He has many questions, but he isn't sure whom to ask. His boss, Tim Murray, the director of technical services, is out of the office much of the time, and when he is there, he is preoccupied with some major changes in the company.

Fred has held several staff meetings, but in these meetings he feels a lack of respect from his subordinates. When he asks a procedural question, he feels disdain for his lack of knowledge about the project under discussion. Twice he has asked his subordinates for reports, and both times, they have been turned in late. He doesn't know if his subordinates generally don't work as hard as they should or if this is a slight to his authority. He is beginning to feel inadequate as a manager and angry and frustrated because he doesn't know where to turn for advice.

What Went Wrong?

1. Tim Murray, Fred's boss, did not give Fred all the information he needed to do the job or tell him where to go if Tim was unavailable.
2. Fred had no mentor or sponsor in the organization to

provide him with a feel for the company. Fred's technical expertise alone was not enough for him to be successful.
3. No one reached out to him to include him in the informal network of the company. Fred was made an outsider.

What Should Have Been Done?

1. The director should have set the tone for Fred's acceptance as the new operations manager. Before Fred came on the job, his colleagues and subordinates should have been informed of his background and qualifications.
2. Fred should have been given the essential information to do the job by a transition person and, even more important, the names of resources available to him. Above all, the director should have made himself available to Fred for information concerning the job or about the organization itself.
3. The director should have introduced Fred to other senior management and set the model of including him in informal meetings, lunches, and other out-of-work social activities that were the norm for the company.
4. The director should have encouraged Fred to seek out colleagues, both white and black, for help on how to be successful within the organization. It was important for Fred to learn how to develop his own network of support, in addition to receiving support from his immediate boss.

What the Director Might Have Said

"Fred, although I've given you much background on the projects you'll be heading, I know it can never be enough. Please feel free to come to me at anytime. I welcome and expect questions. I've also asked Don Stevens in the planning department to be available to you. He's been involved in many aspects of the projects, and he used to work in your department, so he should be an invaluable resource to you. He'll be calling you to help orient you to the company. I know he's looking forward to working with you.

"I may be out of the office a great deal during the next

month, so I want to set a lunch meeting this week to introduce you to some of the other senior staff. I've told many of them about you, and I think you'll be a great addition to our team. There's a group of us who are handball fanatics, and you mentioned that you're pretty good at that, too. If you'd like to be included in our games, let me know. It would be great if you'd join us."

"You're Not Ready Yet"

Yolanda Thompson has been a compensation specialist for a large insurance company for four years. Her evaluations have been excellent, and she is well liked by her supervisor and peers. She has just told her boss that she would like to apply for the opening she saw posted for a supervisor within the personnel department. Her boss knows that she has been taking management and supervisory courses at night and that she has taken advantage of the management development courses offered in-house by the company.

Her boss, June Marlin, who Yolanda always thought was very supportive, discourages Yolanda. "Why would you want to take that job? It's a real headache. So many problems! We're a real family in this unit. I have some things in mind for you, Yolanda. I can really make it worth your while to stay. Maybe I'll see about letting you work on that new procedures manual; also, there's a special one-week training program in Washington that you can go to."

Yolanda persists in saying she is interested in applying because she wants to advance within the company, but she needs her boss's recommendation. Her boss says in a slightly patronizing way, "Yolanda, I, too, want you to get ahead. But I just don't think you're ready yet. You really need more experience here. Also, I'm not sure you can handle the supervisory part of the job. Some of the people in that unit are not easy to handle."

Yolanda thinks, "There are no blacks in the other unit, and June is afraid to take the risk in recommending me for promotion. She doesn't want to rock the boat and get in trouble with the top brass if I'm not successful. But what I don't understand is: I've worked well with her for all these years and gotten excellent performance ratings. Why does she think I won't work out?"

What Went Wrong?

1. June wasn't interested in Yolanda's career development.
2. She undercut Yolanda by saying that she wasn't ready yet without offering any elaboration.
3. June subtly tried to bribe Yolanda by offering her new assignments and a chance to go to a special training session.

What Should Have Been Done?

1. June should have worked with Yolanda on a career path and made sure that she was getting the kinds of experience that would allow her to apply for a supervisory position.
2. She should have reviewed Yolanda's qualifications for the new job in an objective way. Were other people with Yolanda's background, experience, and evaluations offered supervisory positions? If so, she can defend her recommendation of Yolanda. Then it is up to Yolanda, as an individual, to succeed.
3. If there was something negative about the unit for which Yolanda was applying, June could have described it to Yolanda and offered suggestions on how Yolanda could handle any problems that came up.

What the Manager Might Have Said

"Yolanda, I know your work here and the training you've taken to prepare for a supervisory position. I know you can handle the job, and I support your efforts to get it. I want to let you know that there are some real problem employees in that unit. I can give you some good tips on how to work with them."

Coworker Hostility and Stereotyping

Sondra Wilkins is a newly hired black fiscal officer for a large governmental agency. Betty Haskins, a white fiscal officer in the unit, is unfriendly to Sondra and has been from the first day they met. Betty virtually ignores Sondra when she comes into the office and makes snide remarks about her to the other coworkers, some of which Sondra overhears. One day, Joan Bianco, the supervisor, hears Betty discussing Sondra with another worker. "So what's Sondra's background? How did she ever get this job? Two of my friends applied, but I guess they were the wrong color!" Joan says nothing as she walks by.

At a staff lunch meeting, the conversation turns to the news events of the week. A police brutality case involving a black alleged victim is discussed. Betty turns to Sondra and says, "So what do blacks think about this issue? I guess you're ready to string up the cops?" Sondra looks away and doesn't answer. Someone else changes the topic.

At her monthly supervisory session with Joan, Sondra says, "Everything would be fine here, but I really can't take Betty's racist remarks." Joan replies, "Oh, forget it, Sondra. That's just how Betty is. Just ignore her, and don't take it seriously. Focus on your work."

What Went Wrong?

1. Joan, the supervisor, heard and ignored Betty's remarks to a coworker that implied that Sondra had gotten her job only because of affirmative action.
2. Joan discounted Sondra's reactions and feelings about Betty's hostile and provocative remarks during the conversation about a news event.
3. Joan took no follow-up action to deal with the two incidents.

What Should Have Been Done?

1. When Sondra was hired, the supervisor should have extended her strong support to Sondra and introduced her to the other staff, describing her background and credentials. This should be done for all new employees.
2. Upon hearing Betty's negative remarks to a coworker about Sondra, Joan should have promptly called Betty in

for a private meeting and discussed the negative effect of her remarks on the morale and productivity of the work team, as well as on Sondra directly. Backbiting among members of a work unit inevitably has a negative effect, not only on the target of remarks but on others as well. Betty can also be reminded that, in addition to having qualifications that are as good as anyone else's, Sondra has the asset of familiarity with the client population. (Members of the fiscal unit are sometimes asked to make presentations to the community.)

3. When meeting with Sondra, Joan should have empathized with Sondra's feelings, assured her of her full support, and stated that she would take steps to improve the work atmosphere.

4. Joan should have encouraged Sondra to respond to Betty if Betty makes insensitive remarks again on racial issues. Joan could have discussed with Sondra various ways that this could be done without escalating the exchange into a major interpersonal conflict.

5. During staff meetings, Joan should have emphasized to the entire staff that establishing a climate of mutual respect for *all* workers is a high priority for the work team and that behavior that sabotages that goal is detrimental to the unit and will not be tolerated.

What the Supervisor Might Have Said to Sondra

"Sondra, I am glad that you shared your feelings about Betty's remarks. Let me assure you that you are a valuable part of this unit, and I will not tolerate any behavior that makes you or anyone else feel unwanted or not respected. I will speak to Betty and the entire staff about my commitment to mutual respect and a cohesive work team.

"I would also encourage you to speak directly to Betty if she makes hostile remarks in the future. I think that might be helpful in getting Betty to understand the effects of her behavior. I'll be glad to problem-solve with you on how to do this in a way that's effective and that also suits your style."

What the Supervisor Might Have Said to Betty

"Betty, I overheard your remarks to other workers questioning Sondra's credentials. Her credentials are as good as anyone's in the unit and in some ways even better, and I believe she is an invaluable member of the team. I want you and everyone else on the staff to be sensitive to the feelings of others as we interact in our diverse workforce. Maybe you can start by asking yourself how you would feel if someone were to make similar remarks about you. Having us all work together as a productive, harmonious team is a top priority for me, and we must all take responsibility in making that happen. Any behavior that detracts from cohesiveness and mutual respect for every member of the team is not acceptable here."

Summary

Racism, both subtle and blatant, is the major issue for blacks in the workplace. Racism is revealed in many ways: hostile remarks, the assumption that blacks are employed only because of affirmative action, skepticism about black competence for management roles, exclusion from informal networks, and misinterpretation of a direct communication style.

Chapter 4

Asian-Americans

Asian-Americans are the fastest growing group, measured by percentage increase, in the United States, although their actual numbers are still relatively small. In 1990 Asian-Americans represented 2.9 percent of the population, or 7.2 million people, for an increase of *107.8 percent* since 1980.[1] They also have a high rate of participation in the labor force and make up approximately 3.5 percent of the national workforce.[2]

The substantial increase in the Asian-American population has been due primarily to immigration. According to the 1990 census, 62 percent of Asian-Americans are now foreign-born, but there are large numbers of Asian-Americans whose families have been in the United States for generations. For example, only 28 percent of Japanese-Americans are foreign-born.[3]

Although Asia covers a wide geographic area, the Asian-Americans described in this chapter are primarily those whose families originated in East and Southeast Asia. They represent the largest group of people identified as Asian-American on the basis of racial and cultural heritage.

Except for Filipinos, many of whom are Christian as a result of the long-time Spanish influence in their country of origin, the Asian-Americans described here have strong Buddhist and Confucian backgrounds that have influenced their cultural tendencies.

Geographically, of course, Indians and Pakistanis are Asians, and people from India and Pakistan who are living in the United States are also Asian-American and are listed as such by the U.S. Bureau of the Census and in most press reporting. However, because their religion (e.g., Hindu, Muslim, or Sikh), racial background, and culture are different from those of other Asians, primarily those from South, East, or Southeast Asia, Indian-Americans and Pakistani-Americans will not be specifically mentioned in this chapter, although they face many of the problems described here.

Moreover, Indian- and Pakistani-Americans are more likely to be recent immigrants than are Chinese-, Filipino-, and Japanese-Americans, many of whose families have been in the United States for one or more generations. Some issues of concern to Indian- and Pakistani-Americans are treated in Chapter 6, which discusses new immigrants. That chapter also includes references to the new Southeast Asian immigrants and refugees from Cambodia, Vietnam, and Laos.

Despite the enormous range of differences in language, social class, and national history, Asian-Americans share many cultural tendencies. These include strong loyalty to family, community, or work; modesty and reserve; a reluctance to complain or express emotions directly and a dislike of confrontation; respect and obedience to authority; sensitivity to the attitudes of others; and a strong work ethic. Although all generalizations are risky, it can be said that these values are important in Asian-American cultures.

As you would expect, many years spent in the United States can have an effect on these values, and most first-, second-, and even third-generation Asian-Americans are in transition between traditional Asian values and mainstream American ones. Accordingly, the attitudes and behavior of Asian-Americans have a high degree of variability, although most Asian-Americans maintain some identification with their cultural traditions and sensibility.

As growing numbers of second-, third-, and fourth-generation Asian-Americans enter the workforce, many still experience some of the problems that more recent arrivals describe. In fact, one of the major issues confronting these Asian-Americans is that despite years—or generations—in the United States, they are sometimes treated as if they "arrived yesterday."

Voices of Asian-Americans in the Workplace

Many Asian-Americans say that they are rarely considered for top management jobs.

Asian-Americans often feel that they rarely get an opportunity in top management or executive positions. They resent the assumption that they lack interpersonal and administrative skills. A Japanese-American biochemist said, "We're expected to do well in technical areas, be smarter, and take on extra assignments without complaining. Yet we're not rewarded for our achievements because we're not considered leaders."

A Chinese-American biologist said, "We often say to each other that we are technical coolies—that's all we're good for."

A Filipino-American woman who works as a budget analyst in a large manufacturing company said, "Our reticence and discipline are held against us. People think that we can't communicate well and that we can't assert ourselves as managers because our style may be different from mainstream Americans. We're seen only as achievers, accomplishing a given task, but not as initiators or go-getters."

A second-generation Korean-American manager in a computer company said, "I sometimes feel as if colonial exploitation still goes on, in a disguised but often open system of inequality. Yes, we're promoted to mid-level management, but that's it."

Many Asian-Americans say that they are seen as excelling only in science, math, and technical subjects.

According to many Asian-Americans, when they are being selected for employment, they are sought in science and technical areas but not in sales, human resources, or executive-training positions.

Even when an Asian-American does have a job in a nontechnical area, the stereotype often remains. Thus, a second-generation Chinese-American worker who works as a writer in a public relations agency complained that when he participates in an after-work sports group at his company, he is asked to be the group's treasurer, even though he has less training in this area than others in the group.

He said, "Stereotypes—even so-called positive ones—can work to our disadvantage. We should be happy, I suppose, that everyone thinks we're so great at math and science. But that works to our disadvantage. Either we're pegged only for those jobs or, if we're not good in those areas, people think something's wrong with us."

Many Asian-Americans say that others take advantage of them.

Some have reported that they are consistently given additional assignments because they usually accept them without complaining. "Managers like working with Asians," a Korean-American worker said, "because they know we will do whatever we are given. It isn't that we're smarter; it's that *smart* is defined by us as giving it 100 percent of our effort." In addition to being burdened with more work, some Asian-Americans resent the fact that they are seldom offered extra pay for the additional workload. Complaining is not considered appropriate by many Asian-Americans, nor is boasting of one's accomplishments. Therefore, they may not tell the supervisor they are overloaded. A Chinese-American insurance claims specialist said, "Some of us will just leave and look for another job rather than complain to our boss about the way we're treated."

Many Asian-Americans say that they are usually all lumped together as one group.

Most Asian-Americans are deeply offended that their distinctive countries and cultures are not acknowledged. One Korean-American college administrator said, "Everyone assumes that most Asians are Chinese and speak Chinese." (There are actually several Chinese languages.) Other Asian-Americans report that in recent years they have all been assumed to be Japanese.

Most Asian-Americans are offended by the fact that resentment about Japanese business is directed at them, even if they are not Japanese. Of course, Japanese-American workers, too, resent being blamed for Japanese business success and even for World War II. This is especially grating to second- or third-generation American citizens.

Many Asian-Americans feel that stereotypes, which are bad enough when directed at a single group, are even worse when directed indiscriminately. Thus, any Asian-American may be a target of anti-Vietnamese prejudice because of the Vietnam War, of anti-Korean prejudice because he or she is a shopkeeper, or, as just mentioned, of anti-Japanese prejudice.

When reference is being made to a specific individual or to a group of people all of whom trace their families back to one country, Asian-Americans say they prefer to be described by national origin, such as Chinese-American, Korean-American, Japanese-American, or Filipino-American.

Many Asian-Americans say that Americans sometimes misinterpret or take advantage of the nonconfrontational or nonassertive style that is part of traditional Asian culture.

Asian-Americans may prefer to make decisions and to solve disagreements by seeking consensus, conciliation, and harmony in relationships. They may express public disagreement in a polite way to avoid a direct conflict. Thus, if asked in a meeting whether they agree with someone's idea, especially if there is dispute over the idea, Asian-American workers may not take a firm stand out of respect for another's feelings. This behavior can be seen by other Americans as being wishy-washy, showing lack of commitment, or being insincere or weak. Yet, to an Asian-American, being direct and forthright might mean being insensitive to the feelings of others or even being offensive.

A Chinese-American computer specialist said, "We're often blamed for being indecisive. We can make decisions, but we may go about it differently. Usually Asian-Americans will try to reach consensus first, before simply making a decision. We will try to do it without seeming to make the other party lose." A Korean-American merchandising manager said, "If Asians are as indecisive as we're supposed to be, why is it that the Pacific Rim countries—Japan, Korea, Taiwan, and even China—are doing so well in the world of business?"

A Japanese-American engineer said, "The irony is that if we are assertive, it is immediately considered aggressive, probably because of the stereotype that we're passive. We're often put into a bind—seen as too passive or too aggressive."

Many Asian-Americans say that others assume that they are all recent immigrants; they feel they are never considered "real" Americans.

"We are always seen as foreigners because we are Asian in physical appearance and not white," a Filipino-American data-entry clerk said. Even a fourth-generation Japanese-American scientist is often asked, "When did you come to America?" or "When are you going back?" or "Have you been home lately?" A third-generation Japanese-American manager who had never even been to Japan is asked, "Isn't that how they do it in Japan?"

A second-generation Korean-American financial analyst is often told by coworkers that he speaks English so well. Other Asian-Americans complain that they are told, "Oh, you speak [or understand] English very well for a foreigner."

Several second- or third-generation Asian-Americans said they had a very strong desire to "fit in" and to deemphasize their being Asian. Many of these workers grew up in neighborhoods where theirs was either the only Asian-American family or one of a few. Thus, their entire lives were spent in mainstream American culture. It was very painful for them to feel totally American and yet not to be seen that way by others.

A second-generation Chinese-American nurse said, "I'm an ABC [American-born Chinese], yet people at work often seem surprised that I am 'with it.' They somehow expect me to act like I'm a foreigner."

Many Asian-Americans say that the first thing noticed about them is that they are Asian.

One Japanese-American bookkeeper complained that as soon as someone meets her in the office she is asked where the best Chinese restaurant is in the neighborhood. (She was not even Chinese-American.)

"Whenever I go out with people for lunch, they seem to assume that I want to eat Chinese food," said a Chinese-American case manager at a social service agency. "Of course, I like Chinese food," she said, "but it's really annoying to be boxed in about it, especially since I grew up in the United States.

Many Asian-Americans say that harsher judgments are made about their performance than about anyone else's.

Not only is a mistake judged more severely, but often the mistake is explained by a stereotype about Asians. Thus, if a report is not as complete as a supervisor wanted, that supervisor may assume that the Asian-American worker wasn't assertive enough with other workers to get the necessary information or that his or her language skills were inadequate.

Some Asian-Americans report that they are victims of the stereotype that Asian-Americans are always excellent workers. "We're supposed to be the model minority. We are not allowed to make a mistake. Anything less than absolutely perfect is considered a failure or a disappointment, although it would be considered satisfactory if done by another worker," said a Filipino-American accountant.

Many Asian-Americans say that other Americans interrupt them, even finishing sentences for them.

An Asian-American may be in the position of having to contradict the person if the "finished" sentence is not what the Asian-American speaker was going to say. A Korean-American government administrator said, "People are incredibly impatient with me. Maybe it's because I sometimes speak somewhat slower or more deliberately than others, even though my English is very good."

Whereas mainstream Americans consider interrupting an indication of interest and see it as just interjecting, interrupting might be interpreted by some Asian-Americans as showing disrespect or aggressiveness or even as being a power play.

Many Asian-Americans who do speak with an accent say that their accents are not tolerated as are the accents of Europeans.

"Why is it that Irish, French, or German accents are considered charming, cute, or continental, but an Asian accent is often viewed as annoying or difficult?" said a Korean-American telecommunications analyst who has lived in this country for thirty years and still retains an accent. Several Asian-Americans felt that their accents are held against them, even if they speak, write, and understand English perfectly.

Many Asian-Americans say that they are perceived as overly deferential to authority.

Asian-Americans who are still influenced by traditional Asian culture are often especially respectful of authority. At the same time, they may expect that the authority will act in their interest through a trusting relationship. Because of their respect for authority, they may not wish to go against what they perceive as the wishes of the person in authority. Thus, they may rarely say no to a request, even when it may not be possible to comply with it.

Even asking questions may be considered insubordinate, since it implies that the person in authority was not clear—an implicit criticism.

More traditional Asian-Americans might not volunteer for a position. Instead, they might expect a supervisor to recognize their skill and select them for a special position.

Since modesty and self-effacement are valued characteristics in Asian cultures, traditional Asian-Americans can often be penalized in American culture if they do not call attention to their accomplishments.

There is a paradoxical aspect to the attitude of many Asian-Americans toward rank and authority. On the one hand, there is an expectation of cooperation and sharing among supervisors and employees, with a strong emphasis on loyalty to the group. On the other hand, there is an expectation that final authority for decision making rests with the person of rank. Indeed, it is the authority who gives permission for collaborative team efforts.

Many Asian-American women say they are subjected to sexual innuendo, expressed blatantly or through jokes.

Many Asian-American women feel they are perceived as highly pliable and sexually available, a view portrayed in American movies such as *Sayonara, Teahouse of the August Moon, The World of Suzie Wong, Flower Drum Song,* and even *The Deer Hunter.* A Chinese-American office worker said, "Even though some of the movies about Asian women were made over twenty years ago, we're still being called Suzie Wong, Lotus Flower, or China doll. It always makes me very uncomfortable when a coworker says that to me."

Although sexual harassment—and complaining about it—is a problem facing all women in the workplace, it is a special problem for Asian-American women because they may be conditioned by their culture not to complain when they are mistreated. They are also vulnerable because they are seen as pliable.

A different, but equally offensive, view of Asian-American women is that they are manipulative, powerful, or sexually lethal. A Japanese-American lawyer said that if she acts assertively in her firm, she is called The Dragon Lady.

Discussion of sex in public is often considered unacceptable for Asian-American women. "Teasing is okay, if we know you," a Chinese-American woman said, "but in general, we tend to be shy and reserved, at least in public." Casual kissing on the cheek, common in the American workplace, is considered a taboo to many Asian-American women.

Many Asian-Americans say that others do not realize that they experience discrimination in the workplace.

A Japanese-American aerospace engineer said, "Many people have the view that we are not only the model minority but the golden minority—that we're all rich and successful. They don't know that we still face many barriers."

Although foreign-born Asian-Americans face greater discrimination, even first-, second-, third-, and fourth-generation Asian-Americans say they face significant employment discrimination, yet most non-Asians don't accept that as the case. A second-generation Chinese-American marketing manager said, "I thought I would have an easy time in the corporate world. I was a leader on my college campus and a good student. But I've been boxed in by two stereotypes: (1) Asian-Americans don't need jobs—we're 'doing so well,' and (2) at the other end—we don't present the 'right' corporate image."

Many Asian-Americans say that others do not understand the stress they experience.

Because they do not like to complain, some Asian-American workers feel that others have no idea how they are feeling. A Japanese-American social service worker who has lived in the United States for fifteen years said, "We are smiling on the outside but crying on the inside."

"In Japan," one telecommunications manager said, "Japanese people are encouraged to go to a doctor once a year for a check-up. All Japanese managers hope they have something wrong with them, an ulcer or the beginning of a heart problem. These problems will prove that they are working hard. If they have no symptoms, others will think that they are not working hard enough! Some of this attitude may remain with us when we come here to the United States and remain with us as part of our traditional Japanese culture."

Scenes from the Workplace

Taking Advantage of a Good Worker

Tony Fortaleza, a Filipino-American, is a loan officer in a mortgage company. He is often asked by his supervisor if he "wouldn't mind" doing some extra reports because one of his coworkers is out sick or there is a vacancy in the department. He always smiles as he says yes. But after accepting the most recent extra assignment, he begins reviewing his last two years on the job. Nothing seems to be changing. Of all the loan officers, he handles twice as many applications and reports as anyone else.

He is proud of his performance and knows that Barbara Wilson, his supervisor, always counts on him to be quick and accurate and never to refuse extra work.

Last month there was an opportunity for a promotion in the department, with some supervisory responsibilities. No one suggested that Tony apply. Bob, a coworker who had been there a year less, got the job.

The day after he hears about Bob's promotion, Tony applies for a similar position in another company and is accepted. When he tells Barbara that he will be leaving in two weeks for the better job, she is shocked. "Why are you leaving? If you wanted a raise, why didn't you ask for it or apply for the promotion that Bob applied for? I never knew you were dissatisfied. What can I do to make you stay?"

Tony says, "Oh, nothing is wrong. I just want a change." Barbara is devastated because she has never had a worker as excellent as Tony. "What did I do wrong?" she wonders.

What Went Wrong?

1. Barbara assumed that when Tony readily agreed to the extra work, it meant that he was happy to do it and pleased that the supervisor knew of his extraordinary ability to get so much accomplished. "After all, wasn't Tony usually smiling?" And he never complained! What Barbara did not understand was that in traditional Asian culture, it is difficult, if not impossible, to say no to a supervisor. To do so would be disrespectful.

   Complaining is also unacceptable. Traditional Asian cultures emphasize that one is taught to accept what is given and not to reveal negative feelings, especially to an authority figure. Although he harbored deep resentment over his lack of recognition in being considered for a promotion, Tony didn't make his feelings known.

2. Barbara never considered Tony for a promotion. She thought Tony was not the type to be in an advanced position. He was "such a quiet person" and did not take initiative to learn new skills, although he was superb at what he did know. At meetings, he rarely said anything unless asked. Moreover, Barbara thought that if Tony wanted a raise or a promotion, why didn't he ask for it?

   What she didn't realize is that modesty is a characteristic of many Asian-Americans, and Tony thought that his work should speak for itself. He thought that the supervisor would appreciate and recognize his achievements and recommend him for the promotion.

   In American culture, workers usually ask for or apply for a promotion. Many Asian-Americans would be hesitant to do this for fear of rejection. To be rejected would be to suffer humiliation and embarrassment—a loss of face. Thus, it was incorrect for Barbara to assume that if Tony was interested in a promotion, he would ask or apply for it.

What Should Have Been Done?

1. When Tony accepted the extra assignments, the supervisor should have acknowledged the extra work and said

that these special efforts would be recorded in Tony's personnel file, with a copy to Tony. Many Asian-Americans do not like excessive praise, especially in front of others, but a formal note and an acknowledgment in the file would be acceptable and appreciated.

2. Barbara, as a supervisor, should have anticipated the possibility that Tony expected a raise, and ultimately a promotion, because of his superior work. As a supervisor she should have initiated some compensation for the extra time Tony worked.

3. Barbara should know that leadership qualities are not uniform; every leader does not look or act the same. Just because Tony was reserved did not mean that he could not succeed in the more advanced position if given the opportunity. Indeed, his extraordinary work could set a model for all employees if he were in a supervisory position. Effective supervisors generally work harder than their subordinates.

Effective utilization of all employees is the hallmark of an outstanding supervisor, and Barbara should have had a broader view of the strengths of all of her staff. In fact, it can be effective in working with any staff to invoke some traditional Asian-American values such as harmony and responsibility to the group.

What the Supervisor Might Have Said

"Tony, as you know from our performance evaluations, I think your work is exemplary. I am very impressed by your willingness to take extra assignments when needed. You are a crucial part of our work group.

"Our budget is tight now, as you know, but I am putting in for a raise for you. In addition, I am planning to give you additional assignments that will prepare you for promotional opportunities. Also, I would like to send you to the next Supervisory Skills training program, which is offered next month. There will be an opening for a supervisory position in the near future, and you might want to ready yourself for that position. I can't promise you anything, but I would like you to think about your future career goals. I am willing to help you in any way I can.

"Meanwhile, I'd like all staff to inform me about any problems or concerns they might have. Even if it might appear negative, I would appreciate hearing about problems so that I can try to improve our operations. I see this as part of our all being responsible for the working of our unit."

Being a Team Player

Karen Cho, who is Chinese-American, works as a secretary in the accounts department of a large department store. This is a tight-knit unit, and there is a great deal of camaraderie among the staff; workers and supervisors swap jokes and tease each other about the work. The supervisor, Janet Barker, sometimes shows appreciation of workers by putting her arm around a worker's shoulder or even giving a hug.

Karen very much wants to be part of the team, but she feels that she doesn't belong. She is always cooperative when someone asks her to help out, but she just can't get into the informal swing of the office. She came to the United States from Taiwan when she was fourteen years old and her English is excellent, but she still misses certain idiomatic phrases, although she often pretends that she understands. Also, the style of humor is alien to her, and she is very embarrassed by sexual jokes.

She knows others think she is standoffish and prudish, and she feels bad about not being a part of the group. When, after several refusals, she did join the other women for a party after work, she felt very isolated. The conversation dealt with none of her interests, and she didn't know what to say.

She is becoming increasingly uncomfortable at work and keeps more to herself. She is more reluctant to interact with other members of her work group, even when she needs information from them to complete her tasks.

Several times she has made errors on forms because it is difficult for her to ask her supervisor or other workers questions about the instructions.

Karen's worst fears are confirmed at her midyear evaluation. In a forceful manner, her supervisor says that Karen's work has fallen off and that she should work more with the other staff to coordinate her tasks. She tells her to "lighten up" and "get with it" or she will have to give her a mediocre evaluation at the year's end.

Karen is so humiliated and embarrassed by Janet's feedback that she can't even defend herself. She then withdraws even further from the others in the work group.

What Went Wrong?

1. Janet, the supervisor, was unaware that when Karen did not fully understand the job instructions she was reluctant to "lose face" by asking Janet to repeat the instructions. To Karen, doing so might imply that she wasn't able to follow instructions. Also, in Karen's mind, asking questions of an authority might seem to imply that the supervisor was at fault for not making herself clear, which would be an insult to the supervisor.

2. Janet did not realize that being a "team player" in American culture is very different from being a loyal group member in traditional Asian cultures. In the latter, the emphasis is on task accomplishment, a sense of loyalty, and sensitivity to each member of the team. In the American workplace, being a team player often means being part of the informal social atmosphere as well as being cooperative on work issues.

3. Janet did not understand that Karen was uncomfortable about the joking in the office, particularly about the sexual humor.

4. Janet should have realized that Karen might be uncomfortable with any type of touching, even if it was a sign of approval. Thus, Karen certainly would not welcome having Janet's arm around her or receiving a hug. Since they weren't really friendly, Karen might have seen such moves as phony gestures.

   Karen was also uncomfortable when Janet singled her out for praise, especially if it was in front of others. This special attention, separating her from the group, was unusual in her culture and cause for embarrassment.

Traditional Asian culture tends to emphasize "we," not "I."

5. Janet did not realize how sensitive Karen might be to her feedback, which Janet assumed was part of routine supervisory evaluation. Her forceful voice was seen as being aggressive by Karen and caused her to "clam up."

What Should Have Been Done?

1. Janet should have given Karen clear, explicit instructions on each work assignment. She should have tested Karen's understanding by asking for interim reports on the assignments. When giving instructions, Janet should have asked Karen to repeat back in her own words her understanding of the specific task. This is, of course, good supervisory practice for all employees.
2. Janet should have noticed that Karen was not part of the team at an earlier stage of her employment. She should have noticed how uncomfortable Karen was with being touched and how she reacted during work-group horseplay.
3. While not necessarily changing her behavior toward the others, Janet should have been more sensitive to Karen's style. To help her feel more comfortable with the other workers and them with her, Janet could have structured some team projects involving Karen with other workers. When the joking seemed to make Karen uncomfortable, Janet could have changed the subject. Certainly, she could have at least toned down her own joking with Karen. Janet might also have spoken to the staff, suggesting that off-color humor is not appropriate in an office setting.
4. Janet should have given feedback to Karen in a way that would not seem to be criticizing her. She should have helped her to understand the style of the office. While not expecting Karen to change her value system, she could have helped Karen to learn about the office culture here and to adapt as much as she felt comfortable doing. Americans pride themselves on being very direct, but many traditional Asian-Americans pride themselves on

being indirect and believe that criticism should be expressed indirectly so as not to cause embarrassment to either its giver or receiver.

What the Supervisor Might Have Said

"Karen, we value you as a member of our work team and are pleased at how conscientious and cooperative you are in helping others when they ask you for information. I want to talk about several issues, but I think it would be helpful if I explained the feedback process. What I say is not intended as personal criticism or a judgment of you. Rather, it is a way of sharing or teaching you something that would make our team work better without blaming either of us.

"I am concerned about whether my instructions are completely understood by you. As you know, the reports were not completed in the way I expected. This may be because I am not clear enough or because you need to clarify my expectations for a given assignment. There is no value in blaming either of us. What's important is that we do understand each other and find a good way to do this. I would like you to ask me questions on any aspect of the work that is not clear to you. On my part, I will go over assignments periodically so that we both know we are in agreement. I intend to do this with all staff members. It would also be helpful to the team if you request information from the other staff members when something is needed for your work. In our office, speaking up and speaking out are considered virtues.

"Finally, Karen, I know that you do want to feel more part of the team. As a start, I'm going to have you work with Marlene on some of the large reports that the unit has to complete. It might help if you went out to lunch with some of the people in the office. The others would like to be friendly with you, and I hope in time you will feel more at ease with them."

Stress in Maintaining High Work Standards

Sue-Jin Kim, a Korean-American, came to the United States with her family when she was five years old. She is now a financial systems analyst in a large pharmaceutical company. She is assigned by her department head to coordinate work on two budget projects because she has a reputation for being very thorough and is well liked by her peers. Her new assignment involves supervising three men analysts and one woman with whom she had worked as an equal under the direction of the department head.

She is looking forward to the opportunity of demonstrating her abilities as a professional and as a manager dealing with the interpersonal aspects of the project. She knows the stereotype that pegs Asian-Americans as excellent technicians but weak managers. She is determined to dispel that notion and to carry out the new assignment in a noticeably superior way, since she wants to be considered for a senior management position in the future.

She knows from working in the unit that several of the analysts are quite lax about completing their projects on time and are not used to stretching their creativity to come up with something really innovative.

She tries to impress on her four supervisees that she has high expectations for the project and wants their cooperation in submitting assignments on time. Because they are professionals as well as former coworkers, she is reluctant to give them specific directives on how to accomplish each task. When she speaks to them about the quality of their work and her concerns about it, she does so in a rather indirect way so as not to embarrass anyone. Yet one of the analysts calls her "uptight" when she describes her work expectations.

The work that is subsequently submitted by staff members is mediocre. The department head, Pete Merrill, does not seem pleased with the unit's output under Sue-Jin and says so in a very direct, forceful way. Sue-Jin, however, tells Pete that it will take only a little longer to get things going well and that everything is fine.

She then resolves to make up for the slack performance of others and takes work home several nights a week. Not only does she have high standards, she is used to working very hard. She has occasionally been called a perfectionist by several coworkers and supervisors in the past, but this is her work norm and she expects others to have the same standards.

The stress of this new job is beginning to show. She feels humiliated because the staff does not seem to respect her authority and also because she was criticized so forcefully by the department head. She is afraid that she will fail in this new job.

What Went Wrong?

1. Pete, the department head, never prepared Sue-Jin for managing this work unit, particularly in view of the misfit between her perfectionism and the staff's lax performance. Instead, Sue-Jin, a highly skilled systems analyst, was plunged into a managerial position with little briefing and no formal training.
2. Pete's forceful, direct expression of opinion about the work unit was taken as a strong personal criticism of Sue-Jin's managerial skills.
3. He did not realize that Sue-Jin's assurance that "everything is fine" meant that Sue-Jin would not admit having any problems. Sue-Jin believed that if she described the problems with the workers, she would be seen as complaining, which she was not comfortable doing. The supervisor took Sue-Jin's assurance at face value.

What Should Have Been Done?

1. Before being selected for a management position, Sue-Jin should have had training in management or, at a minimum, briefing on how to deal with a work group composed of people who had formerly been her peers and who had poor work habits.
2. Sue-Jin needed coaching on her interpersonal style, which might be perceived as formal or vague. She should have been coached for a somewhat more assertive mode of communication that stressed directness and clarity of expectation, all expressed in a firm manner.

   Likewise, Sue-Jin should recognize her responsibility in giving constructive feedback to her staff whenever needed. She may need coaching on how to give feedback to her staff and help with overcoming her discomfort in doing so.

3. The department head should be involved in staff meetings to share departmental expectations and indirectly to support Sue-Jin.

4. Pete should remind Sue-Jin that his forceful and direct manner is not meant as a rebuke or strong criticism. Rather, it is his style of expressing concern. He should then reassure Sue-Jin of his continued support and confidence.

5. The department head should state the need for openness in their relationship, such as reporting on the negative aspects of the unit and Sue-Jin's problems in dealing with difficult staff. She must be assured that she can speak openly so that together they can work on management issues. She should be told that silence is often seen as approval in mainstream American culture.

What the Department Head Might Have Said

"Sue-Jin, I'm sorry that I failed to brief you adequately on managing the work unit. As we both know, there were productivity problems with all four analysts, and before I plunged you into that situation we should have gone over some strategies for managing them. I think one of the ways we can do this is to have you take a general management course being offered next month. I think this would be helpful to your working in this unit and in your overall career development.

"In the meantime, I would like an ongoing open relationship with you in which you will feel free to come to me with any unit concerns. Let's meet regularly once a week, even if briefly. You are a highly esteemed employee, and we want this to work. We both have a stake in your success.

"And, Sue-Jin, let me assure you that we are not trying to change your basic style of leadership. But you might want to modify your style somewhat to meet the expectations of your workers. A somewhat more assertive stance with firm, clear directives might be a more effective management style for *this* team.

"If you have no objections, I'd like to be invited to attend your weekly staff meetings and then share with you my perceptions on how your directives are heard and how you might overcome worker resistance, if any. This would not be meant to 'watch' you in a critical way, but just to be of help.

"I think we can then work out a management style that is acceptable for you and will have a more effective impact on staff improvement. You and I have a challenge ahead of us, but I think we'll make a good team and meet our objective."

Summary

The workplace examples in this chapter highlight managerial misinterpretations of Asian-American tendencies. Such tendencies, which may affect employment assignments, performance, and evaluations, include reserved communication style, different work norms and values, nonconfrontational attitudes toward authority, modesty, inclusive decision making, and different concepts of team and leadership style.

Chapter 5
Latinos

The terms *Hispanic* and *Latino* are often used interchangeably. There is no consensus on which term is preferable, although *Hispanic* is seen more often in publications and is used by the U.S. Bureau of the Census. However, since *Latino* now seems to be favored among group members, this will be the term used throughout this book.*

Latinos are the second largest and numerically the fastest-growing minority in the United States today. According to the 1990 census, the nation's Latino population is 22.4 million, a jump of 53 percent over the 1980 count. Latinos represent about 9 percent of the total U.S. population.[1] (Blacks represent 12 percent.) Latinos also represent one of the fastest-growing groups in the labor force, increasing 65 percent since 1980, "a rate of growth four times that for the non-Hispanic workforce."[2] As another example of the increasing presence of Latinos, Spanish is spoken as a first language at home within the United States almost twice as much as all other foreign languages combined.[3]

Although millions of Latinos, especially Mexican-Americans, are American-born and come from families who have been here for generations, 41 percent of Latinos in 1990 were immigrants. Another 26 percent were children of immigrants and thus likely to still be influenced by their traditional family culture.[4] Thus, there is some overlap between this chapter and the chapter on immigrants. This chapter, however, focuses on Latinos who are English-speaking and either mainland American-born or acclimated to American society far more than recent immigrants.

Latinos are an extraordinarily diverse group. The term de-

*The term Latina is sometimes used to describe women.

scribes people originally from more than twenty different nations in Central and South America and in the Caribbean, as well as from Puerto Rico, a commonwealth of the United States, and Spain.

In addition to country of origin, Latinos differ in social class, occupation, level of assimilation, and color. Latinos are white, Indian, black, or—most often—a mixture of two or more of these groups. Most black Latinos are from Puerto Rico or the Dominican Republic. Many Latinos from Central and South America are of mixed Indian and European background and are called *mestizos*.

Although most Latinos are Catholic, heavy inroads are being made in some urban areas by Pentecostal Protestants, and many Caribbean Latinos adhere to an African-Caribbean religion called Santeria.

Despite these differences, there is a bond among Latinos, based primarily on language—Spanish—and also on some cultural characteristics, especially a strong emphasis on family and communal ties.

Anthropologists have described two major worldview differences between mainstream Americans and Latinos. First, for Latinos, the primary identification is with family and ethnic group, whereas for mainstream Americans, individual identity is usually more important than loyalty to the family or ethnic group. Second, to Latinos, social orientation focuses on interpersonal relationships, even at work. Mainstream Americans usually separate social and work relationships.

Voices of Latinos in the Workplace

Many Latinos say managers have consistently low expectations of their ability.

Time and time again, Latinos complain that coworkers and supervisors assume they have only the most minimal competence and that they are intellectually inferior.

A typical reaction when a Latino makes a contribution or point that has merit is a look of surprise—even shock—that crosses over the face of the other. After a Cuban-American manager spoke effectively at a large meeting, someone came up to her and actually said, "Is your name really Carmen Gonzalez?" The observer could not reconcile the competence of the speaker with the Latino name.

A Puerto Rican woman who had a management training position in a large consumer products organization said, "When I completed my projects on time, people would seem surprised and say, 'Oh, you did it!' Or when I joined a discussion about a new product or procedure, I'd be asked, 'How do you know about that?' "

Another example of this assumption was given by a Mexican-American who was part of a bank training program. At the end of the first orientation session, the instructor came up to reassure him that she could offer him all the help he needed and that she could arrange for special assistance if this was necessary. She made no such comment to anyone else in the training group, although there were several recent immigrants from the former Soviet Union and from Korea. There is a widespread notion that any Latino in an important position is there only because of affirmative action. While affirmative action might sometimes be the impetus for the hiring, the Latino person is usually qualified and may even have outstanding qualifications for the job, perhaps better than those of his or her predecessor.

Latinos say that others resent their ambitions and efforts to get ahead.

A Mexican-American worker who delivered mail to the professional staff in a large brokerage company was very well liked by the professional workers. Yet when word got around that he was taking college courses and wanted to be a broker himself, several workers suddenly mocked him about it. He felt they were friendly to him while he was a mailroom worker but resented it when he wanted to establish a more equal relationship. He said, "Some of the people seem to think of me as a kind of pet, treating me with kindness but like a child." He wasn't sure whether he was treated this way because of the other workers' low expectations of his ability or because of their desire to feel superior to him.

Many Latinos say that personal relations are ignored in work settings and that only the task is given importance.

For many Latinos, loyalty in the workplace is often to a person and not to the position. The workplace is seen almost as an extension of family, and the personal aspects of a working relationship are very important and are intertwined with the task. Latinos say they must know something about the manager on a personal and human level before they can feel comfortable working with that person. The concept of *personalismo,* which refers to relationships and friendships, is extremely important to most Latinos.

A Puerto Rican social agency manager said, "First there must be a feeling of trust, then we can talk about family and personal ties, and only then can we have a good working relationship." Another Puerto Rican worker said, "We are incredibly loyal to supervisors and other workers once we have a relationship. Sometimes, though, the relationship—the *personalismo*—just doesn't happen. Some people only care about the product, not the person."

An architect who came to the United States from Colombia twenty years ago said, "Of course we recognize the difference between a working relationship and a personal friendship. But even in 'just' a working relationship, most Latinos expect a strong personal component. We have the task and our humanity in common." He added, "Some organizations don't have a culture that allows Latinos to feel comfortable. Many Latinos work best in an atmosphere that is like a family. We like to celebrate birthdays, engagements, holidays. Supervisors have to know this, or they think we are unprofessional or unbusinesslike. We can have personal relationships *and* get our work done."

Many Latino women say they are offended when others see them only as sex objects.

Latino women say they are often viewed as a "Latin bombshell," Chiquita Banana, or another stereotype that demeans Latino women by assuming an "easy" sexuality. Although women in all groups report that they are seen as sex objects, a Cuban-American executive secretary explained, "Most Latino women are extremely sensitive about being considered sex objects in work situations because of the stereotypes about us."

Individual Latino workers or managers do not want to be seen as the spokesperson for all Latinos.

As with any group, there is enormous variation among people regarding any issue. This is especially true with Latinos, because Spanish-speaking people come from so many different areas and have such diverse backgrounds. A Colombian-American physician said, "I realize that people can't know about all Latinos, but they should know that there is a difference between a recent immigrant from a rural area in Ecuador with no skills, a *mestizo* like myself who is a first-generation college graduate, and a third-generation physician from Argentina from a European background. Our interests, needs, and experiences are totally different."

A Puerto Rican city manager with a master's degree in public administration said, "American whites recognize class differences among whites, but they seem to think all Puerto Ricans are the same."

A Mexican-American personnel administrator in a large city said, "Why do people think we know everyone with a Latino name? Coworkers will often ask if I know José Rodriguez or someone with another Latino name. Don't they realize that there are millions of Latinos in this city?"

Many Latinos say that their different cultural heritages are not acknowledged when all Latinos are lumped together.

Such amalgamation denies the differences in national origin. In the Southwest, all Latinos are assumed to be Mexicans. In the Northeast, all Latinos are assumed to be Puerto Ricans. In the Southeast, especially Florida, all Latinos are assumed to be Cuban. Although these groups may predominate in their respective areas, there are also Latinos from virtually every country in Central and South America, as well as from the Caribbean, especially Puerto Rico, Cuba, and the Dominican Republic. Each group takes great pride in its unique background. While there may be an affinity to other Latinos, if only because of the language, there may also be competitive feelings. Each group takes pride in its own national background. That's why individuals usually prefer to be identified by their country of origin (i.e., Mexican-American, Cuban-American).

Also, since Latinos are from so many different racial backgrounds—some are white, some black, some Indian, and many a mixture of two or more groups—they resent being lumped together as if they were all of one race (i.e., whites, blacks, and Latinos). The identity of Latinos is based not primarily on race but on language and cultural factors.

Many Latinos say that others assume that they all come from poor backgrounds and that they all live in a certain area, particularly inner-city urban ghettos.

A housing agency manager of Puerto Rican background who grew up on Long Island in a suburban community and went to an upstate New York college, virtually all-white, said that people always assume he grew up in East Harlem or in a slum in the South Bronx in New York City. He said, "Actually, 40 percent of Latinos live in the suburbs now, but the media insist on showing us as living only in inner-city ghettos. I think this is what makes it hard for us at work. People assume that our life-style is totally different from theirs. Sometimes it is, but often it's not. My college major was business and accounting, but when I graduated, all the good jobs for me seemed to be only in government or nonprofit agencies."

A Mexican-American purchasing director said that people were surprised at how he handled himself at corporate social events. He said, "They fell all over themselves complimenting me on 'how well' I did with the corporate socializing. They seemed to think I would be awkward and not know what to say."

A Puerto Rican social worker who worked in a mental health facility said, "The white doctors always seemed uncomfortable, nervous around me—as if I wouldn't know the right answers to questions. They acted as if they didn't know how to talk to me. It's funny because I grew up in an Italian and Jewish neighborhood and went to mostly white colleges. I wanted to tell the guys, 'Relax. You can talk to me like a normal colleague.' I didn't say anything because I didn't think it would work."

Many Latino workers say they are restricted to working only with Latino clients or customers.

The assumption is made that Latinos' only competence is speaking Spanish or working with "their own." A college-educated Chilean-American was hired as an administrative worker in a hospital personnel office but was given work only as a translator, even when she asked for work in other areas. Numerous Latino workers describe this "tracking system," which often limits their workplace opportunities.

Many Latinos say that many workers and managers expect them to look alike.

Latinos are expected to be conservatively dressed to conform to some kind of business norm. A Mexican-American man in one business setting said, "Why can't I wear a purple shirt and still be seen as a professional worker?" On the other hand, a Latino man in a different business setting, perhaps a government agency, might resent being teased about being so conservatively dressed.

Many Latinos say that others assume that they have nothing of importance to say if they do not speak up at meetings.

In many American workplaces, meetings are considered an opportunity for workers to "show off," that is, to show how smart they are. Many Latinos, in contrast, have been brought up with the belief that when you play yourself up, it's at someone else's expense.

A Mexican-American computer programmer said, "Some people just like to talk and have their say even if they don't have anything new or important to contribute. We speak at a meeting only if a point has not been made, and we're not competitive about being the first to make the point." A Colombian-American first-line manager said, "I consider it disrespectful to speak at a staff meeting when I am the junior person. In my culture, you don't take the 'seat of honor' from the head person."

Many Latinos say that managers and workers assume that all Latinos are late for appointments or meetings.

A Cuban-American department head in a food manufacturing company said, "It is true that time has a different, more flexible meaning in Latino culture than in the mainstream American culture. Latinos agree that it is important to get a job done but that it does not have to be done within an exact time frame."

In some Latino countries, there is a tacit understanding that a 9 A.M. meeting will not actually start until 9:30 or 10 A.M. However, most Latino managers interviewed in the United States feel that it is essential for Latino workers to conform to the time rules set by a given organization and that their cultural norm of not being compulsive about time is inappropriate to a workplace that *is* exact about time. Countless Latino workers get to work precisely on time, a Puerto Rican municipal manager in a major city said. "It's true that Latinos tend to be late for social occasions. But they do know the difference between social time and work time—*if* it's made very clear to them by their supervisors. Anyone questioning Latinos' willingness to get to work on time should observe the New York subways at 6:30 A.M. when the subways are filled with Puerto Rican and Dominican workers getting to their jobs in the garment industry by 7 A.M."

He added, "Because some Latinos do tend to have a different view of time from mainstream Americans, managers should try to be accommodating whenever they can. But if there is a reason for punctuality or if it's the organizational norm, managers should make it very clear what they expect."

Many Latinos say they are frequently criticized by managers and coworkers for speaking Spanish to Latino colleagues.

Employees and managers working with Latinos often complain about the "clannishness" of Latinos. They may be referring to the Latino workers' habit of talking together on the job or at lunch. What the managers may not realize is that Latinos use their common language to relieve the anxieties of the workplace. Speaking Spanish together forms a bond, a feeling of shared heritage and of being part of a family-like group. The purpose of speaking Spanish is usually not to exclude others but to feel comfortable. Latinos resent others' inability to appreciate this need for "togetherness."

A Cuban-American supervisor in the operations department of an insurance company said, "Others should know that we tend to go back and forth in language—Spanish when we're talking personally and English when it's professional."

Scenes from the Workplace

"Tracked" in a Latino Community

Stella Rodriguez, who is Puerto Rican, has been a bank teller in a Latino area for more than four years in a branch of a major bank. She has excellent performance reviews and has taken numerous evening courses offered by the city banking association; these qualify her for an entry position in the accounting section of the operations department of the bank. She sees a notice in a bank communication for job openings in the operations department, which would mean leaving her branch and going to another part of the city. She then speaks to her supervisor about her intentions to apply for the job, since she will need her recommendation.

The branch manager, Clarice Wakefield, is both surprised and annoyed. She is surprised because she doesn't know any Latino women who have worked in the accounting section. She doesn't think Stella can do the work and thinks that even if she can, she wouldn't "fit in" with the other workers. Not only is Stella Latino, but Clarice thinks that Stella's style of dressing is too "flamboyant" for the downtown department.

Clarice is also annoyed because she does not want to lose Stella. The bank needs Spanish-speaking tellers, and Stella is particularly able.

Clarice strongly discourages Stella from applying and implies that she will not recommend her for the position. She says, "Stella, we really need you here to work with our customers. The people in the neighborhood are very comfortable with you. Don't you want to help serve your people? They need you, and I don't think you should let them down."

Stella is very discouraged and decides that she will leave the bank as soon as she can get another job.

After Stella leaves, Clarice complains about the high turnover among the workers in the bank.

What Went Wrong?

1. Clarice seemed to assume that Stella could do only one kind of work. In her experience, she had never seen a Latino woman move beyond being a teller. She made the assumption that Stella was not qualified for the other job and that even if she were able to get the job, she and the others in the department would be uncomfortable working together. Clarice assumed that the other supervisor would not want Stella in the department.
2. Clarice told Stella she was indispensable in her current job because she was Spanish-speaking. She was implying that Stella could not work with other groups, as if there were some kind of unbridgeable gap between them.
3. She was making Stella responsible for the well-being of customers at her own expense. Stella was, in effect, in a dead-end job. Clarice tried to make her feel responsible for whether the community was adequately served.
4. Clarice could be held liable in a discrimination lawsuit, since she was in effect preventing Stella from advancement because of her Spanish-speaking skills.

What Should Have Been Done?

1. As part of her normal supervisory activities, Clarice should have helped Stella learn about career opportunities suitable to her interests and abilities. (Instead, the bank was going to lose a good worker.)
2. If Clarice felt Stella's style of dressing was too flamboyant, she might have told her that the norm for dressing in more advanced positions in the bank is somewhat conservative. Of course, Clarice should question her own standards of dress. While there are parameters of professional attire, Clarice's particular rules may have been very limiting.
3. She could have asked Stella to recommend someone who could be trained for her present position.
4. Of course, she could have notified the bank's personnel

department of her needs, encouraging them to maximize their outreach efforts.

What the Supervisor Might Have Said

"Stella, I didn't realize that you were interested in moving into another department. Together, let's go over your qualifications and review the courses you have taken at the bank institute and see how they might have prepared you for the job that interests you.

"I will be sorry to see you go because you have been a real asset at this branch and to the community, but I understand that you are interested in pursuing and advancing your career, and I admire your ambition.

"If you do get the job for which you are applying, we would appreciate your help in our hiring someone else. If you know anyone who would be interested, please let us know so that we can enhance our outreach efforts in the community. Of course, our personnel department will be working on this, and we will be advertising in the press."

Misunderstandings about Communication Style

Roberto Rivera, a Mexican-American, is a mid-level supervisor in a packaging company. He and his unit always perform well; they meet deadlines and have a good reputation for customer satisfaction. Yet when he has his first annual review, his boss, Jerry Packard, the department head, tells Roberto that he is not a good "team player" and that he shows little initiative or leadership at staff meetings. Thus, his overall rating is "satisfactory" instead of "excellent" or "outstanding." When Roberto asks for specifics, the department head is rather vague.

Roberto is very discouraged and speaks to another worker about the evaluation. The other worker tells him he heard the department head say that he is annoyed that Roberto rarely speaks at staff meetings and then comes up to the department head after meetings to discuss in private his concerns about or disagreement with what had been said during the meeting. The department head apparently feels that this is sneaky, manipulative, and even cowardly; if Roberto has something to say, why not do it in the public forum of the meeting? He feels this behavior shows Roberto is not a good team player.

Roberto, who is almost twenty years younger than the department head, sometimes looks away instead of looking directly at the department head, especially when he is being criticized. This contributes to the department head's idea that Roberto is underhanded.

What Went Wrong?

1. The department head assumed that Roberto did not speak at meetings because he had no initiative and that he expressed disagreement in private because he was cowardly and wanted to curry favor with the department head. Roberto's looking down instead of directly into the eyes of the department head confirmed his lack of directness. None of this was the appropriate interpretation of Roberto's behavior.

2. Several cultural tendencies common to Latinos can explain Roberto's behavior. First, as we have mentioned, many Latinos do not feel that it is essential to speak in public at a meeting unless a point has not been made adequately by someone else. They do not feel competitive about being the first to make the point or, as some might say, "to be heard just to be heard." They consider it polite to let others have their say and then add a comment only if there is something new or important to add. Since he was in a highly competent department, Roberto added to the meeting only occasionally and when a point had not been made by someone else.

   Second, many Latinos do not like to disagree in public and see public disagreement as confrontational. It is seen as rude or disrespectful to disagree in public with the speaker and viewed as almost insubordinate to disagree with a supervisor in public; thus, Roberto chose to speak to the supervisor alone. He did the same with peers in the department with whom he differed, but the supervisor did not know this. Roberto was not cowardly about expressing disagreement; he was doing it in a way that was acceptable in his cultural upbringing.

Finally, Latinos sometimes see it as brazen or disrespectful to look directly into another's eyes, especially when being criticized. This is generally the case, however, with Latinos not born in mainland United States.

What Should Have Been Done?

1. The department head should have expressed his concerns to Roberto earlier in the year and inquired about the reasons for Roberto's behavior.
2. The department head should have coached Roberto on how he could be seen as more effective in meetings.

What the Department Head Might Have Said

"Roberto, I notice that you say very little in staff meetings. Is there a reason for this?" If Roberto explained that he speaks only when he feels it is essential, the department head could have said, "Here it is important to hear from everyone. In effect, we like to count everyone in. If you are silent, we don't know whether this is concurrence or disagreement. In our department, we welcome differences of opinion as long as people act respectfully toward each other. Disagreement itself is not seen as confrontational, if it is expressed respectfully. I prefer that you make your opinion known at our meetings, rather than in private."

Time and Family Issues

Luis Santiago, a Colombian-American, is late again. Steve Ruskin, his supervisor, is exasperated. Luis's work is excellent; the clients in the child-welfare agency like him, and the reports and grant proposals he produces for the agency are outstanding. But twice in the past month, the director of the agency has come into their office at 9 A.M. looking for Luis, who wasn't in yet. The director recently said to Steve, "I can never find Luis. Can't you control your own staff?" Steve explained to the director that Luis is not bound by the clock and stays overtime many nights to help a client. He never asks to be compensated for this. The director said, "That's all well and good, but this agency opens its doors at 9 A.M. sharp, and I expect Luis and everyone else to be here on time."

Steve confronts Luis about his lateness. "Luis, you have been coming in late a lot of mornings and it's got to stop. I know Latinos are casual about time, but the director is really serious about this time issue. Is there any reason you can't come in at nine?" Hesitantly, Luis says, "No, there's no problem. I'll try to make it in at nine." However, in the next few weeks, Luis is late several times again, exasperating Steve.

What Went Wrong?

1. Steve linked Luis's lateness with the derogatory stereotype about all Latinos being "casual" about time.
2. Steve stated his expectations about lateness and asked whether Luis had a problem complying. When Luis said there wasn't, Steve assumed the time issue was resolved.
3. Steve had no relationship with Luis outside of their working together on specific tasks. He did not know about Luis's home situation. Actually, Luis was responsible for his child in the morning, since his wife left for work at 6 A.M. Before leaving for work, he had to wait for a babysitter to come. In addition, he had to check on his elderly mother in the morning. While it was a struggle to get to the office at 9 A.M., staying late was not difficult because his relatives were able to take care of his child and his mother after 5 P.M.
4. Steve did not know that in Luis's culture, family considerations are of primary concern. The welfare of his child and his mother had a higher priority than getting to work exactly at 9 A.M., and he felt that he was meeting his job responsibilities by working late.
5. Since Luis had no personal relationship with Steve, he could not admit that there were family responsibilities

that prevented him from always coming in on time. In Luis's culture, problems are not shared with outsiders.

6. For some Latinos, it is difficult to be directly assertive toward authority figures. It was easier for Luis to be compliant in saying that he would come on time than to say, "I cannot come in at 9 A.M. on days when the babysitter is late." To say this might seem to him to be defiant or insubordinate to his superior.

What Should Have Been Done?

1. The supervisor should have focused only on the lateness issue and not linked the lateness to a cultural factor.
2. Steve should have developed a relationship with Luis that was more than perfunctory and work-related. For Luis, as with many Latinos, personal relationships are just as important as the task. If Luis and his supervisor had a closer relationship, the time problem might have been worked out in a mutually satisfactory way.
3. Steve should have explained the norms of the organization about time. Organizations, like ethnic groups, have a culture, with norms and values. In this organization, punctuality was mandatory.
4. Steve should have stated his appreciation of Luis's work in a very specific way and reminded him of his overall importance to the organization. This personal statement of appreciation might have been a spur for Luis to resolve the issue on his own.
5. If Steve had a personal relationship with Luis, he could have explored the family problems and seen whether he could help Luis find some solutions.
6. If Luis could not work out his problems at home, Steve should have gone to the director to ask for a formal change of work hours so that Luis could work from 10 A.M. to 6 P.M. Organizations are becoming increasingly flexible in work hours for both men and women in response to family needs.
7. If it was not possible for the supervisor to get the director to change Luis's hours and if Luis could not work out his

personal responsibilities so that he could get to work on time, Luis would have to be told the consequences of his behavior in a very direct way. This could be reflected in a negative performance evaluation or, in an extreme case, the possibility of dismissal. The latter seems unlikely in view of Luis's excellent work performance. A more realistic possibility is that Luis's lateness would be held against him if he were ever considered for a high position. This should be made very clear to Luis.

What the Supervisor Might Have Said

"Luis, you are doing an excellent job with the clients, particularly with Mr. Jones, who was a really tough case. Your work with Mr. Jones reflects your tremendous involvement with the clients and the agency. We are really lucky to have you here.

"I also wanted to share with you my concerns about your getting to the office after 9 A.M. fairly often. The director is pretty uptight about time and has been after me lately to see that all of the staff are here from exactly nine to five. Has there been a problem with your getting here?"

The supervisor should pause and wait for Luis to respond here. This behavior assumes that Luis feels comfortable with the supervisor because they have developed a personal relationship.

If Luis describes his situation at home, the supervisor might say, "You might want to think about this and discuss it with your family to see if you can get a backup or do something else when the babysitter doesn't show up on time. Why don't you get back to me in two days so we can talk about it again?

"Luis, this organization has a history and a culture of its own, and that includes strict adherence to coming to work promptly at nine. Coming in late, regardless of the reasons, may have a negative effect on your evaluations and on promotional opportunities. You are such a valuable worker that I would hate to see your lateness lessen your chances of promotion in our organization."

Speaking Spanish on the Job

Sonia Jackson is a competent manager in a catalogue company who is considered caring and understanding by her employees.

Her Cuban-American secretary, Elena Jimenez, is an outgoing, chatty, high-spirited woman. Her work is good, but whenever Elena speaks to the other Latino workers, she speaks Spanish in an animated style.

Sonia sees two problems:

1. Although Sonia is generally pleased with Elena's work, she is very annoyed with Elena's style of behavior and her speaking Spanish to the other workers so often.
2. Another issue is that Ruth, a new non-Latino worker, seems left out of the socializing in the office and looks somewhat unhappy.

Finally, after weeks of doing nothing, Sonia walks into the outer office, hears Elena laughing and talking Spanish with another secretary, and blurts out, "What is it with you people? Why do all of you always sit around and talk in Spanish? This is a place of business, not a tea party." Elena seems very upset and turns away. Sonia retreats hastily.

The atmosphere in the office is now very tense.

What Went Wrong?

1. Sonia waited too long to speak to Elena because she felt uncomfortable about speaking to her about her interpersonal style and her speaking Spanish. She was afraid that Elena would think she was prejudiced against Latinos.

   Because she waited so long, her feedback to Elena was given in a moment of high frustration and anger, rather than being thought out.
2. Sonia was derogatory about all Latinos when she linked the talking problem to "you people."
3. She did not raise the issue of Ruth's being left out of much of the interaction in the office and the perception by Sonia, and possibly by Ruth, of an exclusionary Latino clique.

What Should Have Been Done?

1. The supervisor should have given feedback to Elena at an earlier time on the specific issues of office interaction and

the reactions of others in the office who may feel excluded or even worry that they are being talked about.

2. She should not have put a negative spin on cultural characteristics seen as positive by Elena and other Latino workers, such as warmth, sociability, and camaraderie. Instead, she should have helped Elena see how these positive characteristics might be perceived by others as being exclusionary.

3. Sonia should have reviewed her own views about Elena's style of interaction and her use of Spanish with the other workers. Expecting Elena always to speak English in informal exchanges with other Latino workers during the day or during her lunch breaks is too restrictive and unfairly colors her view of Elena's behavior.

4. She should have spoken to Elena in private about her concerns about Ruth's feeling excluded from what might appear to be an exclusive Spanish-speaking clique. By bringing up the issue in public, she may have appeared disrespectful of the Latino women. She should have involved Elena in problem-solving the issue so that the work unit would be strengthened by having everyone feel included without restricting the Latino women's use of Spanish at times during the day.

5. Sonia may wish to speak to Ruth to explain that the intent of the Latino women was not deliberately to exclude her. Rather, Sonia might explain, they speak Spanish because it is a source of comfort for them during the day. She should encourage Ruth to reach out to the other workers.

What the Supervisor Might Have Said

"Elena, I really think that the relationships among most of the secretaries are excellent. For most of you, there is a great team spirit, and we really value that. But I am really concerned that you conduct most of your interaction with the others in the office in Spanish. There are a few problems for me in this, and I need your advice on a situation that concerns me.

"I understand that it is comfortable for you to speak in Spanish, and that's fine when it's occasional and certainly when you are on your own time, like at lunch. But if you do it all the time, it makes others feel left out. Ruth does seem kind of left out of things, and she doesn't seem to be part of your group. It would be great if you could include Ruth in your interactions more often. I'm sure this would make her feel more like part of the team here. Perhaps you can speak informally to the others about my concerns about having everyone feel included in the work unit. We want everyone to feel comfortable working here.''

Summary

The knowledge and use of Spanish presents two unique workplace problems for many Latinos. One is the tendency of some managers to assign Latinos exclusively to Spanish-speaking clients and customers, and the second is the resentment felt by managers when Latinos speak Spanish to their workplace friends and colleagues. Adding to the language issue is the fact that many non-Latino managers and Latinos have different perspectives on communication patterns, standards of time, and the importance of links between personal and work relationships.

Chapter 6
Recent Immigrants

Immigration has caused some of the most dramatic changes in the workplace over the past twenty years. In 1965, the immigration laws were changed to allow close relatives of legal residents to immigrate and to eliminate barriers based on race. As a result, the 1970s and 1980s rivaled the great period of immigration at the turn of the century.[1]

What's different about the new immigrants is that 84 percent are from Latin America and Asia, compared to about 31 percent before 1965. No longer are the majority of immigrants to the United States from Europe and Canada.[2]

In addition to immigrants, several waves of refugees have arrived in the United States during the past twenty years. These refugees have been granted special status because of political persecution in their native countries. Large numbers of refugees came first as a result of the Vietnam War and later as a consequence of political crises in Central America, the former Soviet Union, and Eastern Europe. From 1981–1990, there were more than 1 million refugees, many from Vietnam, Laos, and Cambodia alone.[3]

Immigrants to the United States between 1970 and 1990 came from the following regions of the world:

Asia: 35.3%
Latin America: 47.9%, including:
   Mexico: 23.75%; Caribbean and Central America: 11.1%;
   South America: 13.1%
Europe: 12%
Canada: 12%
The rest of the world: 3.1%[4]

About 60 percent of these new immigrants and refugees entered the workforce, creating new issues and concerns for management. Some of the refugees have suffered severe emotional traumas that affect their work. Salvadoran refugees, as well as refugees from Cambodia and other Southeast Asian and Central American countries, may have witnessed or experienced violent attacks, imprisonment, or torture prior to coming to the United States. Many may have lost family members or do not even know where their families are.

The recent immigrants bring to America extremely varied backgrounds; they range from the highly skilled and educated to the unskilled and illiterate.[5] Many of the highly skilled have done well in the American workplace, although stereotypes remain. Certain problems are faced by skilled and unskilled alike. These include language problems, underemployment relative to the skills they bring with them, and difficulties adjusting to American cultural styles and work norms. These problems are the focus of this chapter.

Obviously, the new immigrants from Latin America and Asia are facing some of the same problems that confronted earlier immigrants from those regions. The additional problems of the new immigrants are substantial and different enough, however, to merit a separate chapter.

Voices of Recent Immigrants in the Workforce

Many immigrants say they're resented because of the assumption that they are taking jobs away from native-born Americans.

Despite common perceptions, most academic and government studies agree that immigrants help to expand the economy, actually increase the number of jobs available, and fill jobs that cannot be filled by American workers.[6] For example, many immigrants are self-employed or start their own businesses. Immigrants also take jobs that many American-born workers shun. As a Vietnamese garment worker said, "We like piecework because we feel we can get more money for our work, but Americans don't like this kind of work. You must remember, we gave up everything to come here; we want to work very hard to save and send money home."

Many immigrants from South America came to the United States to escape abject poverty. They are grateful to have virtually any job, however menial.

On the other end of the skill spectrum, many high-tech companies and research laboratories are increasingly dependent on highly educated and experienced immigrant scientists and engineers from Hong Kong, Lithuania, India, and numerous other countries, since there is a shortage of native-born Americans in some of these fields. However, while the skills of many immigrants are being utilized, others are still underemployed in comparison to the positions they had in their former country.

Many immigrants say that they are treated as if they are not smart or are in some way inferior because of the way they speak English.

Since most recent immigrants are from Asian, Spanish-speaking, or Eastern European countries, they speak with an accent, and their grammar may not always be correct. Almost all the immigrants interviewed felt that people treated them as if they were stupid because of their language problems. A Cambodian immigrant said that people speak louder to her and pause between words: "They talk to us as if to a child."

"Maybe my language isn't good," said one Russian social service worker, "but my mind is good. We are not simple, because our language is. And few people realize how difficult it is to learn English." This woman, who had been an art historian at a major university, pointed to a Chagall poster in her office. "In Russia, I could have spent one hour discussing and describing that painting. In the United States, even with my relatively good English, I only have the vocabulary to discuss the painting for five minutes."

A Russian chemist said, "Most Americans don't realize how hard it is to think in another language. It is not just the words and grammar that are different—it's the ideas and concepts, too. When I came to this country ten years ago, there was no word for *privacy* in Russian."

Also, there are some words that immigrants aren't familiar with, even though much of their English is good. For example, an immigrant from the Dominican Republic who worked in the cosmetic section of a large department store was asked by a customer for after-shave or men's cologne. She said, "I had never heard of these words but was able to fake it by asking the customer if he could spot what he wanted on the shelf. I remember how upset I felt—always waiting for words I didn't know. Everyone was so impatient with me—other workers, my boss, and the customers."

Many immigrants resent the fact that others require them to speak only English.

Many immigrants said they want to speak to each other in their native language to enjoy a sense of ease, comfort, and familiarity; to relieve feelings of loneliness, helplessness, or exclusion; or to be sure that they understand what it is they are supposed to do on the job. There is so much stress associated with working in a new atmosphere and with struggling in English with coworkers and supervisors that they'd like to speak their native language when possible.

A Laotian worker in a photo-processing company said, "It is considered impolite to speak to people from my country in English, rather than in our own language." Indeed, members of virtually all immigrant groups felt it was appropriate to speak to a fellow immigrant in their own language. Some suggested that to get an idea of how immigrants feel, Americans should imagine themselves working in Japan or Russia, where they would always feel the temptation to speak to other Americans in English.

A Puerto Rican insurance clerk said he sometimes wants to speak Spanish in front of Americans so that the Americans will understand what it's like not to understand the language being spoken. "It gives us a feeling of power. Now *they* know what it's like to be on the outside," one Colombian engineering technician explained. An Estonian hospital worker, trained as a psychologist, reiterated that speaking in his native language brought a feeling of "comfort and power."

Many immigrants say that they're assumed to be inferior, and not just because of language problems.

"After all, wasn't where you came from of lesser value than here? If not, why would you have come?" A bank teller from the former Yugoslavia felt this was an implicit question he often faced. He felt that native Americans automatically assumed they were superior to those who had left their land of birth.

Many immigrants say that coworkers and employers assume they don't want to learn English.

An immigrant from Russia said, "Most of us desperately want to learn English, but the schools have long waiting lists. I had to wait two years before I could take a program in my area." A female immigrant from El Salvador working in the garment industry said, "We came here to do better. We know we have to learn English. But it is hard to work all day, then learn English at night, and still take care of my family." She also described how hard it was even to get into a class in her neighborhood. "Almost everyone I know is on a waiting list."

Many immigrants say that employers make generalizations about their ethnic or national group on the basis of experience with a few workers.

A Polish immigrant working as a placement official at an agency dealing with recent immigrants is often told by employers that they don't want people of a certain nationality. "They had one and it didn't work out!" the official said with amazement. On the other hand, she gets requests for "more of the same nationality" simply because one employee from that group worked out well.

Many immigrants, like other group members, say they are associated with any negative news about their national group.

Latin American immigrants, especially from Colombia, are frequently asked by employers or coworkers if they are related to drug dealers. Russian immigrants are asked about the "Russian criminal ring" operating in New York City or about how to "manipulate the system." The questions are not simple curiosity; often the immigrants feel as if they are being implicated in the negative news, a kind of guilt by association.

Many immigrants say that their education and technical skills are not recognized and are often resented.

An Indian scientist felt that many of his skills were underutilized. "What do we do when we see a boss poorly designing a scientific research project, when we have the Ph.D. and the know-how but are seen as low-level workers?" One of his friends was actually fired when she told her superior that his chemistry statistics were inaccurate. Eastern European, Asian, and Latino immigrants feel that they have to hide their expertise. "It is somehow seen almost as an insult; people are more comfortable with the idea that we're inferior" is how one Russian described this. He, like others, dislikes having to hide his experience to avoid arousing resentment in others.

Many immigrants resent employers' tendency to discount their previous work experience and education in their native country. A Haitian electronics technician said, "Our degrees from technical schools in Haiti and our work experience are seen as worthless. It is only American work experience and education that seem to count. We have to start from the very bottom to prove ourselves, and even then we're not always given the chance to show what we can do."

Immigrant workers feel that little or no effort is made to find out what they actually know and can do. To complicate the matter further, many immigrants are reluctant to speak up about their skills.

Many immigrants resent others' lack of understanding about their tremendous sense of loss.

There are great psychological stresses in being in a new, strange country and culture. There is a major sense of loss—of family, home, social supports, and, sometimes, professional status. A Rhodesian inventory clerk explained, "We lose everything that is familiar in our lives and have to start all over."

Immigrants who were journalists, doctors, engineers, or successful business owners in their native countries suffer attacks on their identity from having to work in jobs requiring little skill.

Many immigrants are perplexed that others have no curiosity about their background. A Cambodian immigrant, working as a technician in a photography equipment company, said, "I saw my parents killed. I was in a prison work camp for years before I escaped. Then I walked hundreds of miles at night to a refugee camp in Thailand—all before I was twenty-three. Nobody knows what I went through to get here." Despite this, or perhaps because of his pleasant, smiling demeanor, most people have no idea of or interest in the enormous sacrifices he's made to establish himself in this country.

Several immigrants felt that managers have no understanding of the family problems they face. In their former countries child care was handled by other family members or, as in the former Communist countries, by a state-run child-care system.

One immigrant worker who saw the movie *E.T.* said, "I understand how E.T. felt. I sometimes feel like I'm from another planet myself."

Many immigrants say that they are considered disloyal or "un-American" if they speak favorably about their native country.

"I miss so much about my life in Trinidad," one immigrant said to a fellow technician in a printing company. The coworker answered, "If you like Trinidad so much, what are you doing in this country?" Sometimes this kind of comment is linked to resentment about immigrants' "taking jobs away." A Haitian immigrant reported that other workers resent her listening to the "Haitian station" on the radio during lunch or on a break. She, like many Haitians, does this regularly to get news about Haiti. When she spoke nostalgically about Haiti, she was told by a coworker, "Since you're always talking about 'home'—as if home were still Haiti and not the U.S.A.—why don't you go back there?"

Other immigrant workers say they are told, "This is your country now; get used to it!" A Pakistani engineer said, "Americans don't recognize the difficult transition we have to make. We want to be good Americans—that's why we came here—but we still have very strong ties to where we grew up. Believe me, my kids are already on their way to being 'real Americans.' They have to have Nike sneakers, and they love McDonald's. I still have a strong sense of belonging to two countries."

Many immigrants say that they are lumped together with people very different from them.

Immigrants from the Caribbean complain that others have little awareness of the differences in the various island cultures. Often, these immigrants' only commonality is their skin color, since most are black. There are large cultural differences among French- or Creole-speaking Catholic Haitians; English-speaking Jamaicans and Trinidadians, most of whom are Protestants; and Spanish-speaking Dominicans, most of whom are Catholic.

Similarly, Asian immigrants feel that Americans do not distinguish among the more than thirty countries from which Asians come, nor do they understand and show interest in the political or economic circumstances that led the Asians to emigrate.

Many immigrants say they are ridiculed or mocked because of the way they dress.

Dress customs vary from country to country, and sometimes adult immigrants are slow to catch on to the "right" way to dress. Their clothing may be notably different from that worn by mainstream Americans. For example, Asians used to an agricultural life may dress very informally, even for a job interview. On the other hand, a Colombian woman was criticized by fellow workers in a cosmetic factory for acting so "high and mighty" because she came to work wearing attractive dresses and high heels (as she did in Colombia, where she worked as a secretary), while the other workers dressed casually in jeans and sneakers.

A Russian physicist explained that he learned painfully, and only through a helpful supervisor, that there are different standards of cleanliness in dress from what he was used to. "No one wants to be considered 'dirty'—that is a universal concept—but what constitutes 'dirty' may vary."

Many immigrants say others have little understanding of their culture and how it affects their work habits and behavior in the workplace.

Many workers from the former Soviet Union say they were not encouraged to be independent or take initiative in their former country. A Ukrainian bookkeeper said, "We saw ourselves as screws or nails—just one piece of a work project. We expected our supervisors to make decisions for us." A Russian computer programmer said, "In Russia, we listened all the time to our boss, our party, our union leader."

Many immigrants from other traditional societies are likely to be reluctant to take initiative on the job. Thus, because of their past experiences, some immigrants from Eastern Europe hesitate to speak up and tell the truth if something is wrong. "If there is a mistake, we don't want the supervisor to notice. We're afraid we'll be disliked or punished. We've been afraid so long that we would rather be in the second row than the first, said a Polish factory worker."

Southeast Asians are also affected by an authoritarian and traditional past. Many Vietnamese expect to be told what to do and are reluctant to ask questions for fear that it would be considered disrespectful. As one garment district worker said, "We do our work the way we think is best if the instructions aren't clear. If our boss wants it done in a certain way, he should say so. Otherwise, we assume everything is okay."

Many immigrants say that their nonverbal behavior is misunderstood.

Many traditional Asian cultures emphasize nonverbal communication, such as subtleties of voice tone and facial expression. To many Asians, to speak in a loud and harsh voice is to be disrespectful and offensive.

A Cambodian mailroom worker said, "We smile to make our boss happy." Often, when employers give instructions or admonitions to Asian immigrant workers, they are not understood. Instead of trying to clarify the communication, the Asian worker may laugh or smile, to the employer's disapproval.

A Filipino machinist said, "We say yes and smile or shake our heads up and down to pretend we understand. It shows our respect, and it's a way to avoid being embarrassed." He made it clear that the intention was not to deceive, although it could be interpreted that way by an American manager.

Ethiopians are sometimes considered shy and humble in the United States because of a soft speaking voice and manner. This cultural style can be misinterpreted as weakness, fear, or even laziness.

Immigrants from the former Soviet Union, too, have a difficult time with nonverbal communication. Many resent being perceived as grim or glum. "In Russia, work is work, all business," a medical technician stated. "In America, everyone smiles—even when you walk into an office and don't know anyone, you smile. It is required. That is hard for us. In Russia, it is expected that we smile with friends, and you are your true self only with friends."

These immigrants perceive "official" smiles to be empty, meaningless, and insincere. "The fast friendships here don't mean anything. It just leads you on," said a Polish health aide. "When you try to respond and be friendly yourself, you are rejected. We don't seem to understand the rules of behavior."

Indians, Pakistanis, and Middle Easterners, as well as Eastern European immigrants, say that others complain that their intonation sounds rude, demanding, harsh, and blunt. They say that they don't mean to be rude but that their speech is often interpreted that way. Middle Easterners also say that they are criticized for speaking too loudly or abruptly.

Many immigrants say that there is too much emphasis on time and punctuality in the American workplace.

For the most part, punctuality was not a work norm in the former Communist countries. There was also a casualness about time. For example, there was an expectation that workers would "clock in" and then take time off during work hours to attend to personal business, such as going to a doctor.

For many Asian immigrants who come from a farming culture, time was also not a major factor. A Cambodian job placement worker said, "Time doesn't mean the same thing to Asians as it does to Americans, if they do not come from the big cities. In rural Cambodia, everyone worked on a farm or in their own business, so hours were self-set and variable." An Eastern European worker said, "We have to get used to making an appointment here to see someone. In our country, you can just drop in to see someone at work. Here everyone seems so busy."

Many immigrants say that American employers don't understand or respect their spiritual beliefs, religious observances, or holidays.

East Asian Buddhists resent being touched on the head. A Cambodian social service administrator said, "This is our high point or the 'High Spirit.' It is deeply offensive for someone to intrude on this sacred, holy spot. American employers or workers don't realize this and will sometimes pat us on the head in a friendly or patronizing way, maybe because some of us are so short."

An Egyptian worker in a manufacturing plant said that he had difficulty observing Muslim holidays because they are not recognized by his company. "So many workers in my city are from Arab or Muslim countries. I wish our bosses would let us take time off on our holy days. We could make up the time, but they don't take our holidays seriously."

A Portuguese immigrant said that he wanted to return to Portugal in August because that was vacation time for all his relatives. His boss insisted that the only time for his vacation could be July; no accommodation would be made.

Many immigrants, especially from Asia and Latin America, resent the "aggressiveness" of their supervisors.

A Dominican hospital aide resents the harsh tone of his boss, who will say loudly, "I don't like the way you did this—do it again!" The recent immigrant said that he expected the boss to say something like "Please do this again" in a pleasant tone. The term *respeto*, loosely translated as respect, is used over and over again by Latino immigrants to mean honor and deference to another person, regardless of his or her status.

Several Asian immigrants say they will simply not return to work if they feel offended on the job because of an "aggressive" boss or coworker. As a Vietnamese worker said, "We just don't come back."

Scenes from the Workplace

Limited English and Workplace Effectiveness

Juan Mendozo, a Guatemalan factory worker, has worked at a company manufacturing machine parts for one year. During this year, he received several injuries on the job and had to take off time from the job. His boss, Steve Dillon, now tells him that if he continues to "mess up" and miss work, he will lose his job.

Juan is very conscientious and wants to continue working at his job, even though it is hazardous work. Because of his limited knowledge of English, it was difficult for him to find work, and he is the sole support of his family. (His wife and infant son are here, living in crowded quarters with relatives, but two other children remain in Guatemala with his wife's parents.)

Steve, Juan's boss, asks Juan if he understands how he is supposed to operate the equipment after Steve does a quick run-through of the procedures. Juan, not wanting to look stupid and afraid of being fired, indicates with a nod that he does understand. Juan is scared and feels inadequate because he does not fully understand what he is supposed to do. There are one or two other Spanish-speaking workers on the floor, but Juan was told firmly that he should speak in English and, moreover, that he should speak only to the boss if he has any questions about the work. However, Juan is reluctant to speak to Steve because he always seems in a hurry, speaks very quickly, and seems impatient with Juan.

One time, Steve yelled at him for making a mistake that could have caused serious damage to Juan. "I thought you said you knew how to do that! Were you lying to me or what?"

Juan is very worried—about getting hurt again, about losing his job, about supporting his family here and in Guatemala, about his wife's adjustment to the United States, about finding less crowded housing. He misses his two sons left in Guatemala, as well as his parents, other relatives, and friends. Sometimes he wonders if he will be able to "make it" in this country.

What Went Wrong?

1. Steve cannot accept that Juan's knowledge of English is limited. He does not understand why Juan would say that he understood the instructions when in fact he did not.
2. Steve did not test Juan's knowledge of the procedures.
3. Steve was unaware of the high anxiety resulting from the tremendous stresses Juan was going through on the job and at home.

4. Steve cannot legally require "English only" if speaking English is not essential to Juan's work.

What Should Have Been Done?

1. Steve should have known that when Juan said he understood the instructions, he didn't mean to lie; he was just too embarrassed to admit that he didn't understand. Juan may also have been afraid to ask Steve to repeat the instructions because he thought that he still wouldn't understand completely and then Steve would be even angrier.
2. To find out how much Juan does understand, Steve should ask him to actually perform the task in Steve's presence. If Juan does not perform correctly, Steve can either show him several times (instead of explaining it verbally) or ask another worker who speaks Spanish to interpret for Steve.
3. Steve should encourage Juan to study English. If the company does not itself sponsor English classes (as some large companies are now doing), Steve should refer Juan to available English as a Second Language (ESL) classes in the area. If the company determines that such classes have long waiting lists, it should consider sponsoring in-house classes.
4. If Steve is in an area of the country where there are many Latino immigrants, he should consider studying Spanish himself so that he can supplement his English instructions with Spanish instructions. He might suggest to the company that Spanish classes be offered, as some companies provide, or study on his own.
5. Ideally, training programs should be in Spanish if the workplace is hiring large numbers of Spanish-speaking immigrants. Workers should, of course, be encouraged to learn English. However, the immediate dangers of not understanding instructions given in English justify special training in Spanish.
6. Juan should be assigned a "buddy" who has some knowledge of Spanish and is highly competent at the job. Steve can also use this worker to acclimate Juan to the job

norms. It will be less intimidating for Juan to learn from a coworker than from "the boss."

What the Supervisor Might Have Said (If Juan understands little English, a translator should be used.)

"Juan, the equipment you are using is very complicated, and it is really essential that you understand all the operating procedures for working the machine. Otherwise, there is a danger that you will get hurt again, and the next time it can really be serious. After I show you how to do it, I want to see you go through the operation. Don't worry if you don't get it right the first time. I am also assigning Dave, who works next to you, to help you if you have a question. Since it's important for you to speak English here as much as possible, I want you to work primarily with Dave, who speaks some Spanish. If Dave isn't here and you feel that you might get injured or do some damage because you don't understand something, then talk to Jaime in Spanish. We do want workers to speak English here, but it's even more important that we avoid injuries and produce a good product."

The Underemployed Worker

Galina Popov, a Russian physicist, emigrated to the United States five years ago. Despite a satisfactory knowledge of English and a doctorate from a prestigious science institute in Moscow, she was unable to get a job in any way related to her former work. In desperation, she settled for employment as a technician in a large optical company.

Katherine Harris, Galina's boss, has a difficult time dealing with Galina. She often asks for feedback on her performance, even though the quality and output of her work are excellent. Galina also asks questions about procedures or optic theory. Katherine finds Galina's frequent questions and requests annoying and intrusive. When Katherine does try to be friendly and discuss theoretical aspects of the work in response to Galina's inquiries, she thinks that Galina is condescending and implies, by her tone of voice and attitude, that she knows more about the field than Katherine does. What bothers Katherine most of all are the repeated suggestions Galina makes about various aspects of the work. This makes Katherine feel that Galina is trying to undercut her authority and show herself off as the expert.

Galina feels cut off from her boss and her fellow employees. She knows she has a serious demeanor and is generally not comfortable with small talk. She wants to have relationships with her coworkers and feels they will respect her if she shares her knowledge with them. Although everyone smiles at her and appears friendly, no one has suggested going out after work during the entire two years she has worked at the company.

For Galina, the work is dismal—no challenge and no sociability and certainly no acknowledgment of how much she contributes to the workplace.

What Went Wrong?

Katherine has little understanding of Galina's immigrant background, particularly her experience in Russia, and how it affects her behavior on the job. The issues that Katherine needs to understand are the following:

1. Galina strongly feels a loss of status and prestige in working at a job where her talents aren't utilized.
2. Galina is intellectually curious and wants to talk about the theory of optics and the rationale behind technical procedures. She wants to be helpful to others and thinks that her suggestions will enhance her status as a knowledgeable employee. She does not realize how her frequent questions and suggestions are perceived by Katherine.
3. There is a paradox in Galina's behavior that is not uncommon in underemployed immigrant professionals. Although Galina knows she has superior knowledge and skills, she is also extremely insecure in the workplace. This is a carryover from her former totalitarian country, where employees were afraid of making a mistake. She is also worried that she could be fired here, and she is the sole support of her family and knows it is difficult for

immigrants to get jobs. Thus, she has a constant need to ask, "How am I doing; is it all right?"

4. Galina, like many Eastern European émigrés, wants to socialize with coworkers but is uncomfortable with the "instant intimacy" that is the American norm, an intimacy that seems insincere when there is no follow-up. Galina did try to be friendly and was disappointed that the smiles and small talk of her coworkers ended at the workplace. There was no attempt to involve Galina in after-work socialization, which is a norm in her native country.

What Should Have Been Done?

1. Katherine should have acknowledged Galina's expertise when she was hired. Although she could have empathized with Galina on her inability to get work in her field, Katherine could have stated the strengths and limitations of this job and any possible ways Galina's expertise might be used.
2. Katherine should reassure Galina that it is not necessary constantly to ask for feedback, since she has been doing a good job. Galina should use her own judgment about her performance, and, if anything is amiss in her work, Katherine will certainly let her know.
3. When Galina repeatedly gave suggestions on work improvements, Katherine should have told her that although the suggestions were welcome, she would prefer to have them in writing. Galina should be told that frequent interruptions in the workplace are not acceptable, since they make it difficult for Katherine to do her work.
4. Katherine should spend some time with Galina, perhaps at a structured meeting where she could give Galina feedback on her performance and review Galina's suggestions and decide with her which could be implemented. This attempt at mutual problem-solving would not only acknowledge Galina's status and performance but might also actually improve the workplace.
5. Katherine might suggest to the other employees that they include Galina in some lunch or after-work socialization

because Galina is new to the workplace (and the country) and might welcome socialization with her coworkers.

What the Supervisor Might Have Said

"Galina, I appreciate your interest in our procedures and your obvious knowledge of optics. You seem eager to give me suggestions for improvement and I appreciate that. Could you, however, put them in writing? Make some notes for yourself, and then next week we can get together and look at the suggestions.

"At that meeting we will also have a chance to talk about your work, which is really excellent, and your future plans. Let me assure you that if there are any concerns on my part about your work, I will always let you know.

"I have suggested to the staff that next week, after work, we all go out together. I hope you'll join us. It would be a good way for you, me, and the team to get to know one another better."

Religious Differences and Differences in Communication Style

Waheed Khan emigrated from Pakistan seven years ago and is now working as an engineer in a software company. He is not happy on the job and feels that his coworkers and the senior manager, Joe King, are not happy with him. Most of the other professional workers don't seem to understand anything about Pakistan. Some simply refer to him as "the Indian," having little knowledge of the difference between India and Pakistan. Others who know he is a Muslim think he's an Arab and directly or indirectly assume he may be sympathetic to terrorist activities.

Whenever there is a political crisis or event in the Middle East, there are comments made to him about the "terrorist Muslims." Moreover, coworkers and his supervisors do not understand that, as a religious Muslim, he must pray at certain times during the day. When he took his lunch late one day so that he could be at a nearby mosque at 1:30 P.M. for the regular prayer session, one of the other engineers teased him: "What are you always doing at that crazy hour at the mosque? Praying for that madman Saddam Hussein?"

Waheed is embarrassed and insulted. He wants to explain himself but doesn't want others to think he is strange and different. Since he is deeply religious, he feels a real conflict about explaining his religious beliefs to workers who might ridicule him.

He is dreading the annual Christmas party because he expects to be teased mercilessly. As a Muslim, he doesn't drink liquor or dance. Like many Muslim men, he will not even shake hands with women.

He is a very conscientious and capable worker. In Pakistan he had been the manager of a computer factory, but here the full range of his engineering and managerial experience is not acknowledged. He learned that unless the experience is gained in the United States, it seems to be discounted. Nevertheless, he is eager to prove himself and work his way up the ladder. He is grateful that at least he is working as an engineer.

His relationships with fellow workers are getting him down, and the manager of his work group seems unaware of any of his problems. When he goes to the manager, Joe, he is quite angry about several of his coworkers' having teased him for being Muslim. He speaks to the manager in a loud and forceful voice. Joe is not sympathetic and tells Waheed that it is rude to speak to him in that tone of voice. Joe tells him to work out his own problems with his fellow workers if he wants to stay on the job. If he doesn't, he might have to leave, and he certainly will not be given a recommendation for future work.

What Went Wrong?

1. The manager should have been more sensitive to the fact that there was a problem between Waheed and the other workers, the result of Waheed's background, which was notably different from that of the other employees. Joe should have been aware of some of the stereotyping that Waheed would be subjected to.
2. The manager had no knowledge of the Muslim religion and its requirements, especially about the need for daily prayer. He also had no knowledge about the cultural style of people from Pakistan.

3. He was harshly critical when Waheed raised his voice, since he assumed Waheed was being rude. Joe didn't realize that Waheed was speaking in his typical tone of voice for when he gets upset and that Waheed did not mean to be insubordinate or rude.

What Should Have Been Done?

1. When Waheed was hired, he should have been told by the manager that if there were any problems, he should let the manager know. Joe should have emphasized that this was particularly important because Waheed's background and culture were different from those of the other employees.
2. Since the company is likely to continue to hire immigrants, the manager should become aware that people from other countries may have different values, behaviors, and styles, especially when they have been in the United States for a relatively short period of time. While he doesn't have to become an expert on the background of all employees and their countries, the supervisor should at least be aware that the new American may act differently from typical American workers. Thus, he might ask Waheed if there is anything special he, the manager, should know about Waheed's background that an American might not be aware of, such as rules against drinking or dancing. He should emphasize that he wants to understand any differences in behavior.
3. Knowing that different styles can create communication problems and conflict among workers, the supervisor should make it a point to tell all workers about the importance of understanding and accepting some of the differences and to emphasize that ridiculing someone because of his or her background is not acceptable behavior.
4. The traditional December holiday season can be used as a time to have workers share some of their traditions. For example, at a staff meeting Joe could have explained Waheed's Muslim traditions regarding drinking and danc-

ing so that when Waheed didn't participate he would not be made to feel uncomfortable or be subject to teasing. Or Joe could have encouraged Waheed to explain his traditions.

What the Supervisor Might Have Said

"Waheed, I understand there are some problems between some of the employees and you. Most of us don't know much about Pakistan or about the Muslim religion. I know that you don't want to stand out and seem to be different, but since you do have a unique background it would be helpful if you explained some of this to me and to your coworkers. I am also speaking to everyone about the importance of trying to understand different styles, backgrounds, and religions.

"I also want to give you some help on our customs and styles. In our culture, speaking in a loud tone usually makes you sound angry or rude. When you speak that way, the other person is likely to feel offended. That can cause problems. I know that it may mean something different to you, but I want you to know your tone and loud speaking are different from the way most of us speak to each other."

Summary

Lack of understanding of the background, religious beliefs, and culture of recent immigrants undermines their effective utilization, regardless of their educational status or skill level. Limited proficiency in English is also a key workforce issue, as are differences in verbal and nonverbal communication styles.

Chapter 7
Workers with Disabilities

Out of the 43 million Americans with disabilities, approximately 14.6 million are in the working-age group from sixteen to sixty-five. However, only 29 percent of this working-age group are working, and of those who do, most work part-time or irregularly.[1]

As a result of the 1990 Americans with Disabilities Act (ADA), it is expected that the number of workers with disabilities in the workforce will increase substantially. This law, which became effective in July 1992, bans discrimination against disabled workers who can "perform the essential functions of the job" and requires employers to make "reasonable accommodations" for this group of workers.

The definition of disability is expanded beyond what is clearly visible, such as blindness or use of a wheelchair. The ADA defines a disabled person as anyone with a physical, mental, or emotional impairment or a history of such. Thus, the definition of the term *disabled worker* includes, among others, anyone with epilepsy, diabetes, cancer, HIV infection, AIDS, paralysis, hearing or speech disorders, mental retardation, or emotional illness. People recovered from alcohol or drug abuse are also included.

The implication for the workplace is that a new group of qualified workers is emerging. Of the 4 million disabled workers currently working part-time, many may move into full-time employment. In addition, there are more than 6 million other disabled persons who can easily be made employable with aggressive recruitment and some accommodation.

Barriers to successful employment of workers with disabilities are both physical and attitudinal. The cost of removing barriers or providing special devices, most feared by employers because of the "reasonable accommodation" requirement of the law, is actually far less than imagined. Experts say that 70 percent of the accommodations cost less than $500 per person, and 31 percent cost nothing.[2]

The most formidable barriers, however, are attitudinal, and this chapter will primarily address those barriers, largely limiting the scope to issues that are faced by most workers with disabilities. These issues are managers' and coworkers' discomfort, ignorance of appropriate "etiquette," failure to acknowledge abilities, and unwillingness to make any accommodation. What people with disabilities most want others to understand about them is their need to feel independent and respected for the skills and motivation they bring to the workplace. They want recognition of the fact that they may need special accommodations so that they can perform their job, and, most of all, they wish to be seen as whole persons and not to be defined solely by their disability.

All managers should become familiar with the requirements of the ADA, which are only touched upon here.

Voices of Workers with Disabilities

Many workers with disabilities say that they are not seen as whole persons but are defined by their disability.

"I am blind, but that does not define the whole of me. And yet to most people, that is the only thing that seems important." Variations of this theme were constantly repeated in interviews, followed by statements such as: "I am a director of a small social service agency, a husband, and a father. I go to concerts regularly. I work out at the local gym twice a week. I have many interests. Yet when people talk to me, they seem stiff and ill at ease. Why can't people talk to me about whatever it is that people talk about at work?"

Many workers with disabilities say that they are not seen as capable.

"Others consistently underestimate what we can do," a compensation specialist claimed. Most disabled workers feel that the disability is simply a barrier that can be hurdled and not a total limitation on their abilities. A bookkeeper who is hard of hearing said that when she first started working, other workers seemed embarrassed by her hearing aid and her request to look directly at someone so that she could lip-read. The other workers gradually recognized that she had a different "manner" or "style" of getting her work done but that once minor accommodations were made, she could carry out the full responsibilities of the job as well as anyone else.

Consistently, workers with disabilities say they are not given the full range of assignments, particularly those leading to promotional opportunities, because of assumed limitations on their ability to perform. At an extreme, a personnel assistant said, "If you have a disability, people think you don't have a brain."

Sometimes supervisors are unwilling to provide ongoing feedback as they would to a nondisabled worker, and this creates a barrier to increased job performance. An accounting assistant who uses crutches and a wheelchair said, "They feel sorry for us, so they sometimes give us unwarranted praise. Perhaps that is because their expectations for us are so low. But this is unfair, because then we don't learn, and this is used as an excuse to either fire us or hold us back." This worker had difficulty with a new supervisor because a previous boss had given her exceptionally high ratings, whereas the new manager was highly critical of her work. She said, "It would have been much more helpful to me if I had gotten real feedback and assistance instead of a good rating [from the first supervisor] if I didn't deserve it."

Many workers with disabilities say that employers don't consider them for advancement because they think disabled workers should consider themselves fortunate even to have a job.

A highly skilled toolmaker who uses a wheelchair said that employers expect disabled workers to "be thrilled to be employed." Because of this attitude, "there is never any thought about promoting disabled workers to supervisory positions, even if they are seen as achievers." A payroll clerk said, "If we're not promoted, it's hard to tell if it's because they think we should be so grateful to have any job or because they have doubts about our ability."

Because of the reality that it is difficult for workers with disabilities to find employment, many of these workers are reluctant to ask for promotions once they are employed, and management is satisfied to take advantage of this concern and keep them at their entry level. Another explanation given by a hearing-impaired computer programmer is that "some of us are used to being overprotected and sheltered. Our expectations for ourselves may be too low, and this makes it difficult for us to assert ourselves, and managers may be content to leave us right where we are."

Many workers with disabilities say they are patronized, pitied, or treated like children.

A blind receptionist at a large federal agency says that she and others are often addressed in tones and words that one uses with a child. For example, she is addressed as "honey" or "sweetie" in the high-pitched tone that one uses with a child but not with an adult of equal status. "It seems as if we are treated as lesser people," she said. People who use wheelchairs complain that others pat them on the head—again, as with a child. Some do it condescendingly; others seem to think it is funny—although it is *never* seen this way by the person in the wheelchair.

Many workers with disabilities say they are called courageous and brave unnecessarily.

A legal assistant said, "Why do others assume that we are superhuman or remarkable? We simply do what we have to do to get along in this world productively. Especially for those of us born with disabilities, making adjustments and adaptations seems natural and not extraordinary at all. We don't want to be considered 'special' because of the disability. Our goal is to be seen like everyone else." A magazine writer who was born with spina bifida and who walks with apparent difficulty using arm crutches is annoyed when others commend her for "getting around so well." She said, "I want to be commended for my work and my abilities and not for dealing with the disability, which I take for granted. Most people with disabilities don't want sympathy or undue admiration. We want to be seen as equals in the workplace."

A different outlook was expressed by a manager whose legs had become paralyzed several years earlier as a result of a skiing accident. Perhaps because it was so new for him, he said, "co-workers and other managers aren't sensitive enough to the tremendous compensatory activities that disabled workers use to participate in the workforce. I have learned—through being disabled and meeting many other disabled people—about the beauty and strength of the human spirit that helps us to keep going."

Many workers with disabilities say that they are seen as very dependent.

Most workers with disabilities take great pride in their independence. A blind social worker said, "I was trained from infancy to be very independent, so I was annoyed when a job interviewer asked how I will get to work—an illegal question under the ADA, incidentally. Getting to and from places is a basic issue that I deal with all the time. Of course, there are sometimes problems in logistics or arrangements, but that's something I plan for and know I have to deal with. And besides, many people have trouble from time to time in getting to work—car problems, a broken leg, a sick child."

Because being independent is so important to people with disabilities, these workers are dismayed when people rush in to help when it isn't necessary. Virtually all disabled people prefer to ask for assistance themselves or to be asked whether they need assistance. Thus, a person in a wheelchair should not be pushed without being asked. A person who is blind should not be assisted into an elevator or into a home without first being asked whether assistance is needed and, if so, how it should be done.

Of course, people with disabilities may need accommodations or assistance. A blind supervisor in a social service agency said that the most helpful thing to her was having her first supervisor say, "I've never worked with someone who is blind. Since I want us to work well together, I need you to share with me what I can do to make us work well. What is it that you need so that you can do your job?" The worker said she wished everyone would say something like this.

People with disabilities say that their disability is sometimes seen as a general sign of weakness or illness, even though the disability is often limited to one condition.

A computer analyst who uses a wheelchair because he was paralyzed by a gunshot wound in a robbery says, "Maybe it's because hospitals use wheelchairs to move patients around that people associate wheelchairs with an ongoing illness or disease, but there are so many reasons for wheelchair use—paralysis from an injury, polio, spina bifida, muscular degeneration, or even extreme cases of arthritis. Most of these have nothing to do with other ongoing illnesses."

Many workers with disabilities say that others whom they hardly know ask them very personal questions about the disability.

Personal questions are considered intrusive and embarrassing. "I shouldn't be asked anything that someone else wouldn't be asked," said a word processor who is paraplegic. Yet one young man who is legally blind was bombarded with questions from coworkers when he was first hired. "Were you born that way?" "How did you get to work?" "Do you live alone?" "Who does your shopping for you?" "Do you go out with girls who see?" An employment counselor who uses an electric scooter because of paralysis in her legs was asked, the first day on her job, how she goes to the bathroom. Once a close relationship is established, a disabled worker and a coworker may feel free to ask each other personal questions.

Some workers with disabilities do prefer that people ask them questions directly as long as it is done in a tactful way and the questions are not overly personal. A payroll programmer who uses crutches said, "It is sometimes obvious to me that somebody is dying to ask me something but is just too embarrassed. I would rather be asked a question and then decline to answer than not be asked at all. I find that people will either ask someone else or will make up an answer on their own that is frequently inaccurate."

Many workers with disabilities say that others shun them in informal settings and don't include them in social activities.

A paralegal recovering from cancer said, "Sometimes I think we remind people of their own vulnerability. It's as if people are superstitious. If they associate with me, maybe this will happen to them, too. Casual acquaintances at work who used to be quite friendly seem to stay away from me now." A college office worker with cerebral palsy said, "People seem awkward or uncomfortable talking to us informally at work. They seem to assume that our lives are totally different from the lives of people without disabilities. People are often surprised to hear we are married, have families, and go shopping. A lot of people assume that we have no sexuality, so people seem to avoid conversations about relationships."

Many workers with disabilities feel that so much of being effective at work depends on informal contacts and cooperation that when people shun them or are uncomfortable in their presence, this in itself can be a barrier to being successful on the job.

"I feel that I am not always included because people don't know what's involved if I come along," a worker who is blind said. "The easiest thing is when people just ask, 'What should we know when we go out to lunch together?' Sometimes I'll ask to hold onto someone's arm and have someone read the main items on the menu—this seems to make things easy for all concerned."

Many people with disabilities say that others are too self-conscious about the words they use.

A blind attorney said, "Coworkers will say, 'I'll see you later,' and then they'll apologize profusely. But people in wheelchairs will even say to each other, 'Look who just walked in.' " He explained, "These words are part of everyday language, and we understand that. We wish people would just relax with us more."

People with disabilities say words that are offensive to them are those that have negative implications about the disability and reinforce stereotyping.

"The general rule is to emphasize the person and not the disability." This was said countless times. People don't want to be referred to as "the disabled." Instead, someone should be referred to as "someone who has epilepsy" or "a person who uses a wheelchair."

Language usage has changed, and it is often helpful to ask

about terminology. For example, people who have difficulty in hearing are sometimes referred to as "persons with hearing impairment," and many of them find this terminology acceptable. Some people, however, object to the term because "impairment" seems too negative; they prefer to be referred to as "someone who is hard of hearing." If someone has no hearing, he or she can be described simply as "a person who is deaf." Because terminology does change, it is useful to ask someone with a disability what term he or she prefers.

Many workers with disabilities say that others often speak for them or else discuss them as if they were not present.

Instead of talking directly to a person in a wheelchair, a coworker might say to another coworker, "I don't think Ben can fit into the doorway, do you?" One worker said, "That is an utter wipeout. Why don't they just ask me directly, 'Do you think your wheelchair will fit into the door, or is it better to go down another way?' "

A graphic artist who is deaf works in a large catalogue company and has a supervisor who can use sign language. If she is standing next to the interpreter, however, others will speak directly to the interpreter and not to her, despite the fact that she can lip-read if someone is facing her directly, speaks slowly, and keeps his or her hands away from the face.

Numerous workers with disabilities of all kinds offered variations on this idea: "We want people to speak directly to us. We feel as if we don't exist when people ignore us."

Many workers with disabilities say that others are very impatient when talking with them and don't seem to want to go out of their way at all to understand or to be understood.

An engineer with cerebral palsy said that sometimes coworkers pretend they understand him when they don't. "I know my speech is slurred and that it may be hard to understand. But if someone doesn't understand me, they should just tell me. I don't mind repeating, if people at least make an effort to listen." Another side of the issue of mutual understanding was raised by a hard-of-hearing accountant. He sometimes asks others to repeat what they said if he didn't "get it." Often others will say, "Never mind, it's not important." He feels that it's insulting to him. "It implies that I am not worth repeating for." While complicated or lengthy communications can be done in writing, he misses the normal interaction that takes place between workers because some people are reluctant to take a little more time with him.

Many workers with disabilities say that others don't know basic issues of "etiquette" in dealing with them.

People who are blind say that others sometimes shout at them. "Because we are blind doesn't mean that we can't hear," said a blind receptionist. Another worker said that people don't introduce themselves and make their presence known or say when they are leaving. This worker said, "Imagine how embarrassed I was when I kept talking and found out from another worker that the person I was talking to had left the room."

A lawyer in a wheelchair had several suggestions about the etiquette for interacting with people in a wheelchair. "First, I wish people would not talk to me at length while they are standing; my neck really hurts after a few minutes from having to look up. Second, if someone wants to assist me over a curb or up some steps, he or she should be sure to ask me how to handle the wheelchair and if I prefer to go forward or backward. And never, never, push my wheelchair unless you ask if I need help."

Many people with disabilities say that employers frequently say that it is "just too difficult" to employ them.

Apart from having concerns about workers' abilities, many employers anticipate unwarranted obstacles to hiring workers with disabilities, especially if they have not had any experience with such workers. "I guess we have to become better at explaining just what it is that we need or don't need to make it possible for us to work," explained a corporate manager of administrative services who has multiple sclerosis.

Figures compiled by The President's Committee on Employment of People with Disabilities say that 31 percent of accommodations needed involve no cost, 50 percent cost less than $50, and only 11 percent cost more than $1,000. A data entry operator who is sight-impaired said that she had to have the desk layout changed from the right to the left—at no cost. A headset for a phone allowed a customer service representative with cerebral palsy to talk while she was writing—at a cost of $50. Fewer than 1 percent of accommodations cost more than $5,000, but even these unusual cases may be cost-effective expenses.

An architect with muscular degeneration was no longer able to use his hands for drawing plans, but a voice-activated computer allowed him to continue preparing advanced design blueprints. The cost to his company was more than $10,000, but it allowed a highly experienced professional to continue employment. Turnover costs—not to mention disability payments if the worker were to remain unemployed—made the change clearly worth the cost. Some of the types of "reasonable accommodations" required by the ADA include: accessible facilities, job restructuring, modified work schedules, changes or additions of equipment, and adjustments of job exams.

A director of diversity at a *Fortune* 500 company emphasized that there are an enormous number of governmental (city, county, state, and federal) and private resources for assisting employers in making necessary accommodations. She added, "But one of the most useful resources, often overlooked, is the person with the disability."

Many workers with "invisible" disabilities say that they are conflicted about making their disabilities known because of anticipated negative reactions.

"Invisible" disabilities can include cancer, heart disease, emotional illness, HIV infection, or AIDS, among many others. Often workers with such disabilities are reluctant to discuss them with an employer or supervisor because they are concerned about the possibility of being stereotyped. "It would help us do our job if we knew that they are sympathetic and could help us in dealing with problems that come up. I am still concerned about the stereotyping about mental illness and am reluctant to mention my background to my boss." This comment was made by a chemist who had several brief hospitalizations because of extreme depression. He has now recovered but still requires ongoing therapy. Occasionally he has difficulty concentrating, although he is always able to compensate for these occasional lapses by working late or taking work home. He has difficulty asking for time off to see his psychiatrist because he is concerned about being stigmatized.

Many workers who are mentally retarded say that supervisors are too impatient with them.

A mentally retarded housekeeper in a large hotel chain said, "My supervisor wants me to work much faster. She doesn't understand that it takes me a little longer to do the work, but I can be as good as anyone else. And besides, I never miss a day's work like some of the other people, and I always come on time."

Supervisors often don't recognize that it takes these workers longer and they may need extra supervision. However, "reasonable accommodations" under the ADA requires modifications such as giving instructions slowly and with repetition and offering periodic supervisory reinforcement and follow-up. These supervisors don't acknowledge the long-term payoff in loyalty and reliability once the disabled worker masters the tasks.

Scenes from the Workplace

Sensitivity to a Worker Who Uses a Wheelchair

Jim Jackson, who is paraplegic and uses a wheelchair, is a training specialist in a large chemical company. At a staff meeting, his supervisor, Donna Leland, and some coworkers are discussing the possible use of an off-site meeting room for an upcoming training seminar. Donna and some of Jim's coworkers talk across the table to each other, ignoring Jim completely. Donna, the supervisor, says to Dolores, a staff member, "Do you think Jim's wheelchair will fit into the entrance to the room?" Dolores replies, "I'm not sure that he'll be able to manage it, but we can make a try of it." Donna agrees. "We can try, but it's not going to be easy. If it doesn't work out, though, we don't all have to go."

What Went Wrong?

1. Donna, Jim's supervisor, did not include Jim in the initial planning for the training site.

2. The supervisor talked around Jim, instead of addressing him directly. By ignoring him, she was treating him as a "nonperson."
3. Donna and the other staff member showed their annoyance at the extra effort involved in accommodating Jim at the training site when they said, "We can try, but it's not going to be easy." Even worse, they implied that Jim did not even have to be present at the training event if it was too difficult to accommodate him.

What Should Have Been Done?

1. Donna, the supervisor, should have spoken to Jim about the use of the training site and its accessibility for disabled workers at a very early stage in the planning process.
2. Donna should have addressed Jim directly at the meeting.
3. The supervisor should have made it clear that Jim's presence at the training program was as important as any other employee's.

What the Supervisor Might Have Said

"Jim, I'd like to discuss the training site now that we have the programmatic issues settled. Do you know the conference room at the United Trust building? We were told that the entrance and rooms are accessible for anyone with a mobility impairment, but I think we should check it out. If it's convenient, could you go with us this week to check it out? If it's not convenient, could you give us a list of what to look for? We are planning to check entrance ramps, doorways, elevators, restrooms, lobby phones, and eating facilities. Is there anything else we should consider?"

Needs of a Worker with a Hearing Disability

Lois Miller is a senior data specialist in the accounting department of a health maintenance organization. Ralph Johnson is her counterpart in the MIS unit who knows Lois from having seen her at interdepartmental meetings. He has been told several times that she has a hearing disability, but it is not visible to him from her interactions with others, and he never has spoken directly with her.

Ralph needs quick confirmation from Lois on some data for a deadline he has to meet. As he approaches Lois's office, he meets her in the hall, which is quite noisy with people and duplicating machines. "Oh, I'm so glad I caught you here," Ralph says. "I need confirmation on these reports." Lois looks perplexed and says in a somewhat unclear voice, "Let's go into my office and talk about it."

Once in the office, Ralph buries his head in the packet of materials and hardly looks at Lois as he explains the problem. Lois is straining to look at his face and finally says, "I'm sorry, Ralph, could you please repeat what you said or perhaps write it down?" Ralph, embarrassed, says in a loud voice, with broad gestures pointing to his papers, "It's pretty complicated. I'll go back to my office and write down what I need." He makes a hasty retreat, feeling embarrassed and annoyed at the situation.

What Went Wrong?

1. Ralph began talking to Lois in a hall, which was noisy.
2. Ralph buried his head in his materials instead of looking at Lois, who was able to lip-read if facing someone directly.
3. Ralph did not repeat himself or ask Lois for feedback on whether his request for information was understood.
4. Ralph spoke in a loud voice, using broad gestures, which is not helpful and is often offensive.

What Should Have Been Done?

1. Ralph should have communicated with Lois in a quiet area, such as her office. Noises from walking, multiple conversations, an air conditioner, or photocopy machines are distracting to someone with a hearing disability.
2. Ralph should have looked directly at Lois, and he should have spoken slowly and clearly, particularly if the information was complicated. Lois could then have lip-read at least most of what was said.
3. Ralph should have avoided gesturing unless he was using

sign language. Talking in an overly loud voice is usually nonproductive and embarrassing, since it draws attention to the person with the hearing disability.

4. Ralph should have asked Lois if she understood his request for information.
5. Ralph should have written down what he needed when they spoke and not have left the room so quickly.
6. Ralph should have been aware of his own nonverbal behavior, which showed considerable annoyance.
7. The company, like an increasing number of others, might consider offering sign-language classes.

What Ralph Might Have Said

After making an appointment to meet with Lois in the privacy of her office, Ralph should have looked directly at her as he spoke. "Lois, I'm Ralph from the MIS department." Speaking slowly and clearly, he might have continued, "I need confirmation of these reports. Can I explain what I need verbally, or would it be better if I write it down?"

Appropriate "Etiquette" with an Employee Who Is Blind

Mary Howard, who is blind, has been a receptionist at a large high-tech company for more than two years. One day, walking with her cane to her desk, she passes Jane Fisher, the new advertising manager. Jane very solicitously takes Mary by the arm and in a loud voice asks Mary, "Can I help you back to your desk?" Mary is startled but says, "No, I am fine. You must be Jane, the new advertising manager I met yesterday when you were being introduced to everyone."

Now it is Jane's turn to be startled. "Aren't you sweet? You remembered who I am. That's so nice. You must have a sixth sense. Let me tell you, I think you're wonderful. What courage! It must be so hard for you to do your job."

This time, Mary is clearly annoyed. "I'm doing just fine," she says. What she is thinking is, "It's so discouraging to have people patronize me. I'm just doing my job like everyone else, and doing it well."

What Went Wrong?

1. Jane spoke to Mary in a loud voice, but Mary is not hard of hearing.
2. Jane grabbed Mary's arm without asking; she assumed that if Mary was blind, she needed assistance.
3. Jane was overly solicitous and patronizing in her remark about Mary's being so courageous. She referred to a "sixth sense" that does not exist.
4. Jane did not introduce herself before speaking.

What Should Have Been Done?

1. Jane, the new advertising manager, should have reintroduced herself, since she had just met Mary the day before.
2. She should have assumed that Mary was competent and independent, since she had been on the job two years.
3. She could have described something about herself and her location in the office.
4. She should have talked to Mary as she would have to any other person in the office, in a natural, unself-conscious way. Patronizing or pitying behavior is usually resented.
5. If Jane left Mary first, she should have said so. Otherwise, Mary might have continued talking with nobody else present.

What the Advertising Manager Might Have Said

"Hi, Mary. I'm Jane, the new advertising manager. We met yesterday when the office manager introduced us. I'll be working in the second office to the left as you enter through the doors. I'm in a different spot from the previous advertising manager. I expect to be asking you for lots of information about this place, since you've been here a while, and if you need my help in any way, please let me know. I better get back to my office now, but I look forward to being in touch with you."

Interviewing the Worker Who Is Disabled

Edgar Kramer, who has a neurological disorder and is wheelchair-mobile, is being interviewed for an accounting position in the corporate headquarters of a manufacturing company. He has had experience in both for-profit and nonprofit organizations.

The interviewer, Patricia Baker, begins the interview by saying, "I want to tell you, Edgar, that I have no discomfort whatsoever in dealing with handicapped people. But I am curious to know why you are in a wheelchair. What happened to you? Have you always had this problem?" Edgar gives a short reply, but when Patricia wants to continue talking about his "history," Edgar says, "I'd like to talk about the job requirements and my qualifications, if that's okay with you."

As the interview continues and Edgar describes his qualifications, Patricia says approvingly, "It sounds like you are very qualified to do the work, Edgar. However, how will you get to work? And on your last job, how often were you out of work for illness or doctor's appointments?" Edgar reassures Patricia on both issues, and the interview ends.

Two weeks later, Edgar gets a phone call from the personnel department of the company informing him that they have hired another applicant who was "more corporate."

What Went Wrong?

1. The interviewer was insensitive when she said, "I have no discomfort in dealing with handicapped people." In saying it at the beginning of the interview, she pointed out that the disability was salient to her. Second, the word *handicapped* is no longer used because it has negative connotations of being held back.
2. Immediately asking someone about the details of a disability is too personal, even rude.
3. The interviewer violated several aspects of EEO law, as well as the ADA legislation, when she asked how the interviewee would get to work and whether he would miss work because of his disability. Moreover, until Edgar directed the conversation, the interviewer didn't describe the essential aspects of the job and explore whether Edgar's background would qualify him for the position.
4. Saying that Edgar wasn't "corporate" without any further explanation implies that Edgar—perhaps because of his

disability—doesn't fit a stereotypical image of what a person who works in corporate headquarters should look like. This could be considered discriminatory, as well as insensitive.

What Should Have Been Done?

1. Patricia should have been familiar with the ADA and should have known which questions are illegal during an interview.
2. The interview should stress the job requirements and the applicant's ability to meet those requirements, not the disability.
3. Issues regarding accommodations necessary to enable the applicant to perform the job should be discussed after it is clear that the job can be performed adequately.
4. The interviewer should have known the appropriate language and etiquette to use in addressing persons with disabilities.

What the Interviewer Might Have Said

"Edgar, I am impressed with your background and credentials, which meet our prerequisites for being considered for the job. Let me describe the essential functions of this particular job so that we can see if you're qualified for it." After describing the job functions, the interviewer might add, "Is there anything you would like to ask about the job?" This would allow Edgar to bring up any special issues about how he might best perform the job.

The interview might be concluded with, "Thanks for coming in. We will be notifying you by the end of next week about our decision."

Accommodating a Worker with AIDS

Linda Bailey has been a sales representative for a national clothing company for eight years. Three years ago, when she applied for additional life insurance, she discovered that she was HIV-positive. She assumes she became infected through the blood transfusion she had during a difficult Caesarean delivery of her son. She hasn't told anyone at work, but during the past six months she has had to miss work several times because of illnesses and visits to the doctor. After her most recent illness, she found out that she has AIDS. She doesn't know how to handle the situation because she works in a conservative organization. Although she knows that there is an AIDS policy statement supportive of workers with AIDS, she doubts the sincerity of the policy and is fearful of other workers' reactions and also of losing her job. She knows that she has to speak to her boss if she is to stay on the job at all.

Linda has a meeting with Frank Connelly, her boss, and tells him that she has AIDS but wants to continue working as long as she can. Frank seems uncomfortable in speaking to Linda but does tell her, "Don't worry, Linda. Our company has a good policy for helping workers with AIDS. Just do the best you can, and we'll support you." The meeting is brief, and Frank is worried. Although he has received a company policy statement, he hasn't had any training on AIDS and is not really sure what to do. He is worried about the reactions of some of the workers, but he is a sympathetic supervisor and assumes that he will "just have to carry her and make accommodations with the other workers." After Linda has several extensive absences, however, other workers grow annoyed because they feel Linda isn't carrying her weight, and resentment is building against Linda because of her absences with vague excuses about "illness." Frank doesn't know what to do, and Linda is becoming increasingly uncomfortable.

What Went Wrong?

1. Frank's company has not prepared him for dealing with an employee with AIDS. He suspects that if other workers found out about Linda, they would become upset and want to avoid all contact with her in the office. He may or may not be correct about this.
2. Because he was so uncomfortable in discussing AIDS, he didn't work out a strategy with Linda for accommodating her work to her illness.

What Should Have Been Done?

1. Frank's company should have had an AIDS training program for supervisors and for workers to convey actual

facts about AIDS and to describe the company policy regarding employee protection and supervisory responsibility.

2. If there had been a company policy, Frank would have discussed with Linda a different, less strenuous kind of job and urged her to keep him informed about her illness so that they could work together to keep her on the job as long as possible. This should have been offered only because Linda was not able to continue her work at the previous level.

3. Frank should have known that under the ADA, an employee with AIDS or HIV infection has to meet performance requirements, just like any worker with a disability, but that reasonable accommodations have to be provided. These can include a flexible work schedule, leaves of absence, and job restructuring or reassignment.

4. Frank should have assured Linda of confidentiality, but he might have encouraged her to share the knowledge of the illness with other workers so that they could be supportive. If workers are informed about how AIDS is transmitted and understand that there is virtually no threat to their health through casual contact in an office, workers are likely to be supportive.

What the Supervisor Might Have Said

"Linda, I am very sorry to hear about your illness, but I am glad that you came in to tell me about it. This way, I, as well as the company, can be as helpful to you as possible. Let's work out a plan to adjust your assignments on an 'as-needed' basis so that we can make the necessary adjustments for doctors' visits and absences."

Summary

Attitude and accommodation—and their overlap—are the most important issues in successfully integrating the employee who is disabled into the workforce. Managers and coworkers need to deal with their discomfort and/or annoyance, understand basic "etiquette," and adhere to legal accommodation requirements.

Chapter 8

Younger and Older Workers

Workers are often classified into three age groups: the *baby-busters*, younger workers in their twenties (born after 1964); the *baby-boomers*, in their thirties and forties, born from 1945 to 1964; and *older workers*, those past fifty. This chapter focuses primarily on baby-busters and on older workers.

Demographers and most economic forecasters have predicted a shortage of young, entry-level, skilled workers in the 1990s.[1] The low birthrate from 1964 to 1974 (the "baby bust"), which was only half the post–World War II peak (the "baby boom"), has resulted in a huge decline in the number of sixteen- to twenty-four-year-olds entering the workforce.

Some of the predicted shortages did not materialize because of the economic downturn in 1991–1992. As the economy improved, however, young skilled workers were expected to be a scarce commodity. Because there is likely to be intense competition for this group, managers need to understand younger workers' values, styles, skills, and needs.

Overall, the workforce is aging dramatically.[2] The literature for human resources professionals often refers to the "graying" of the workplace. In 1976 the average age of workers was twenty-nine; by 2000 the average age of workers will be thirty-nine. By 2000, 51 percent of the workforce will be between thirty-four and fifty-four; between 11 and 13 percent will be over fifty-five. These numbers will vastly increase after 2000 with the aging of the baby-boomers, the largest group of all.

One implication is that older workers will be increasingly

important in maintaining a productive economy, especially in light of the predicted shortage of younger workers. Yet stereotypes, discrimination, and underutilization of older workers are barriers to their full contribution.

Managers must also be concerned about this group because of the strong antidiscrimination protection afforded workers over age 40 by the Age Discrimination in Employment Act (ADEA) (passed in 1967 and amended in 1978 and 1986). Although many companies and organizations, for-profit and nonprofit, have tried to avoid lawsuits by offering (some say "pushing") early retirement instead of firing, future workers, now baby-boomers, may be more aggressive in establishing their rights under the ADEA.

Age diversity is also increasingly an issue in the workforce as different age groups work together. In many organizations, hierarchies are "flattening," meaning that teams work across departmental, status, and age lines. Thus, a forty-year-old advertising manager might be working in a team with a twenty-five-year-old computer specialist and a sixty-two-year-old marketing executive. In such cases, the importance of understanding one another's different perspectives is essential.

The differences among different age groups reflect a major transformation in American culture during the last forty years. The older worker's view of the world was clear. Rules and regulations told them where they stood. The environment was safe, government was a friend, employers were loyal to workers and workers to them, ethical structures were clearly defined. Men made up the majority of the workforce. Work was proof of mastery, competence, and moral character. A job was central to one's life; conscientiousness and respect for work and the workplace were givens.

Most younger workers view the world differently. Rules and regulations have no meaning in themselves; they are to be continually questioned. The environment is not safe; the government is not a friend; employers, even nonprofit ones, will not necessarily be loyal to workers; morality is situational. Work, for most younger workers, has no intrinsic value in itself. Work has meaning if it provides self-fulfillment and/or monetary reward. "I do what I want to do because it gives me satisfaction," said a twenty-three-year-old teacher.

In general, younger workers feel "entitled," something older workers never felt. The recession of the early 1990s, however, brought with it an erosion of the "I want it now; I want it fast" mentality of the baby-busters. How this group will reconcile its need to move fast, be fulfilled, and "have it all" with the uncertainties of a downwardly mobile society will be an evolving story of the decade.

The recession has affected older workers, too. Just as more and more older workers seek to continue working, either full-time or part-time, they are finding that they are being fired or urged to retire early or are not being fully utilized.[3]

Voices of the Younger and the Older Workforce

Many younger workers say that managers expect their decisions to be respected solely because they are in positions of authority.

Many younger workers see no intrinsic value in boundaries established by hierarchy, position, and authority. They respect others because of the expertise and knowledge they bring to the workplace or because they can be personally helpful. Younger workers are often not intimidated by status; they want to speak out at meetings and do not defer to "authority." They will find ways to jump across bureaucratic lines to speak directly to someone higher in the organization, especially if they feel their immediate supervisor doesn't deserve to be supervising them.

A twenty-five-year-old assistant to an editor reported proudly that she told her thirty-two-year-old boss, "I don't see why I should take orders from you. You're only a few years older than me, and, frankly, I think I know as much as you do about editing."

They may resent supervisors who want to approve "every little decision" even when the younger worker is highly competent. A twenty-eight-year-old investment broker said, "We're never part of the decision-making process. We're just affected by the results of the decisions. You have no control. Junk flows downwards."

Many younger workers say that information related to the workplace is withheld from them or that they are excluded from activities related to their jobs.

"Work is thrown at us, with no explanation of the bigger picture. We always feel as if we're on the outside," a public relations manager complained. For example, she prepared the background material and picture slides for a meeting and then was not invited to attend the meeting, even though she knew more about the material than anyone else.

Younger workers feel entitled to know "the whole picture" and to be part of the entire process, from decision making to implementation. A twenty-six-year-old assembly worker said that he feels he has no real goals. He's told, "Just get it done." Deadlines are set, but "we know they're not real. They're just moved up, because we're not to be trusted to meet the real deadline. Why shouldn't we think that only money matters in the job? We're nothing to the factory head."

Several young insurance company workers complained when their office space was totally changed around; desks were re-arranged in a seemingly arbitrary way. No explanation was given, and they were rebuffed when they complained. Although all the workers affected were upset, the younger workers were especially furious.

Many younger workers say that they are expected to "pay their dues" before receiving promotions.

Many resent being expected to do the same job for a certain length of time before being promoted or given a raise, just because their superiors had to do it that way. They become infuriated when a boss says, "When I was your age, I would have been thrilled to be in your position!"

Many younger workers say that they are not given sufficient feedback, training, or direction.

They expect their supervisors to let them know how they are doing on the job—the good as well as the bad. For this genera-tion, being ignored is one of the worst things that can happen. Yet many younger workers report that they receive virtually no feedback on work performance until their first performance evaluation, except for an occasional negative remark.

Many younger workers feel that in general they do not receive enough supervision. A young graphic designer said that he wants to learn more about the business, but there seems to be little commitment to on-the-job training. He's in a bind. He isn't given direction or training to do the job, but then he's criticized when things aren't done the way the boss wants them.

A twenty-five-year-old assistant in a printing factory complained that most new workers are not given enough instructions and are not trained; then, when a mistake happens, it is considered the worker's fault. He added, "We are blamed and yelled at if anything goes wrong. I feel like I'm garbage. They treat us with no respect."

Many younger workers say that they do not agree with the notion that work has intrinsic value.

To many younger workers, work is important only if it will help their personal growth or achievement. They see work as valuable because it can be an enriching experience or because they can reap financial rewards. A twenty-six-year-old product developer said, "We want work to be fun, or, if it's not fun, then we at least ought to be making a lot of money." Work for work's sake, as an ethical or moral value, is an alien concept.

An investment analyst, twenty-eight years old, left a senior executive job because he wanted a more "meaningful experience." He was tired of the "drudgery" involved in his work and felt that it had no social significance. Many workers feel that if their current job doesn't work out, it doesn't matter. They'll try something else. This attitude may be changing as the labor market remains stagnant.

Many younger workers say that they lack credibility, despite their knowledge and expertise.

A young woman, executive assistant to the mayor of a large city, said that she is frequently perceived as the secretary. People will come into her office and say, "I want to talk to someone important."

"Wet behind the ears," "just has book knowledge," "callow"—these are all phrases used to demean younger workers despite the reality of what they know and can produce. An assistant director of marketing said, "If we are assertive and describe what we can do, we're seen as brash and pushy. Yet if we don't speak up, we're seen as ineffective. If we're too friendly, we may be seen as socially available."

Many younger workers say that they are not given credit for their work.

Frequently, a young worker will write a report, doing all the necessary research for it, yet the boss will get total credit for it. Since advancement is based on visibility, not getting recognition for work is seen as grossly unfair.

Many younger workers say that they are treated like children instead of professionals.

Young workers resent being compared to supervisors' children and being called "kids." One twenty-nine-year-old credit manager was told by her boss, "Oh, none of you kids want to stay late. My daughter's always complaining about her boss and the time pressures. In my generation we didn't watch the clock."

Many younger workers say that they are criticized too much for their cynicism and lack of loyalty.

Although many younger workers are cynical and do not have strong loyalty to their employers, even these workers feel that loyalty and commitment are two-edged swords. "We are not committed," said an editor at a major publishing company, "because we know that the company has no loyalty to us. With all the mergers, acquisitions, and cutbacks, we are nameless numbers. When new management comes in, we are totally expendable." Another young worker stated, "We are cynical because we've seen people in top management sacrifice workers for an immediate gain in the balance sheet. We look out for us, just the way the companies look out for themselves."

A twenty-two-year-old entry-level management trainee said, "We didn't invent the dog-eat-dog mentality; we just accept it as reality. Then we're the ones criticized for being cynical."

Many older workers say that their experience isn't acknowledged or appreciated by workers younger than they are.

A fifty-year-old training director of a large municipality complained that her experience was discounted as being of little value when a revised orientation session was planned for new workers. Her suggestions were ignored or rejected. The new personnel director told her, "We're going to do things differently around here—more up to date." Ironically, after the orientation proved unsuccessful and the personnel director received complaints, he then asked the training director for advice.

Older workers often feel that their judgment and ability to see the "long view" are not appreciated. For example, a sixty-two-year-old manager in a social service organization was chided for being overly cautious when he objected to sending a "hostile" letter to an official in a public agency. The younger workers in the unit viewed him as too timid, even calling him a "wimp" for not "standing up" to the agency. Yet the manager felt that the agency, a potential source of funding, could hurt their organization at some future time. He said, "Facts are not the whole picture. We have a clinical eye that combines facts with experience. I know that the world is round and what looks like a strength in the short run can end up being weakness in the long haul."

Many older workers say that younger workers are uncomfortable supervising them.

A fifty-year-old city planner was interviewed for a job by a manager in his thirties. The younger man said, "I feel we should be trading places. You should be on this side of the desk. I just wouldn't feel comfortable with you working for me, and I certainly don't think that I could ever supervise you." These blatant statements would, of course, be grounds for filing a complaint for age discrimination, but variations of this scenario were reported many times.

Many older workers say that others have an attitude of disdain toward them.

"We are treated as if we don't know what's going on, are out of it—*clueless*, as the younger workers would say."

One senior advertising executive said, "It's very hard for many younger workers to hide their contempt. They assume we don't know about the 'real world'—often just because we miss a reference to a current pop star or a new TV show. Just because we may not be up to date on popular culture for the twenty- and thirty-year-olds doesn't mean we don't keep up with our professional information. Our attitudes are different on some issues, but different doesn't necessarily mean inferior, as some young workers imply."

An even stronger complaint concerns judgments made on appearances alone. Before any words are even spoken, impressions are made. "You can see in someone's eyes when you are first introduced that you're dead in the water just because you're seen as old," a female marketing manager said. Many older workers refer to "the look" on someone's face as they are introduced. A fifty-seven-year-old accounts supervisor recounted that on meeting someone in another department she was told with a tone of disappointment, "Oh, you have such a young voice on the phone." A sixty-year-old secretary said, "I often feel as if we're judged not on how we think or act but only on how old we look."

Many older women workers say that they are seen as unattractive and nonsexual.

"I have to dye my hair, look immaculate and super-stylish, just so that I am not considered an old granny and somehow of less value. In this culture of youth, we can easily be made to feel somehow extraneous," a senior woman executive complained.

An employment counselor who thought she was being help- ful suggested that a sixty-year-old woman seek employment in a doctor's office: "Doctors' wives like older women because they know their husbands would never make a pass at you."

Many older workers say that they are often compared to younger workers' mothers or fathers.

A training director in her late fifties conducted a seminar for middle managers, most in their mid-thirties. Commenting on the training director's remarks about communication styles, one young woman said disdainfully, "Oh, my mother would say the same thing."

In another instance, at a lunch break, the conversation turned to travel. A young man, sitting next to the training director, said,

"Oh, my mother likes to travel, just like you." Although the remark was essentially a neutral statement, the training director felt that the maternal reference demeaned her professional relationship with the trainees. Instead of being seen as a valued consultant, she was seen as "the mother."

Even when there is no direct reference to a mother or father, older workers resent being seen as parental figures. "We are seen as disciplinarians who set parameters and rules, even when this is a normal part of supervision," a fifty-six-year-old director of purchasing said. "Perhaps we are too abrupt sometimes, but, frankly, I sometimes get tired of having to give reasons and explanations to younger workers on why we have to do things a certain way."

Many older workers say that younger workers consider them drudges, workaholics, or "time-nuts."

"Many of us are Depression babies," a sixty-year-old fiscal director said. "We feel work is work—it is not supposed to be enjoyable. If it is, that's good—but unexpected. We were taught that we have to tolerate frustration; we have to earn a living to support a family."

"Punctuality, reliability, stability, organization—these are the values of the older worker," said a sixty-two-year-old banking manager. Yet these values are considered negatives or are viewed as relatively unimportant by some younger workers.

Many older workers say that they are not given adequate opportunities for training in the latest technologies, particularly computer technology, and that others assume they can't learn new things.

An executive secretary said, "Many of us are willing and able to learn new skills if given the opportunity. Yet if company training is provided in computer technology, it is given to the younger workers. Then, later, we are penalized for not knowing the new technology. It's kind of a no-win situation." This complaint was heard widely.

Older workers also resent the assumption that they do not seek new challenges and promotions. "At age 58, I still see myself growing and developing. I welcome new opportunities and challenges. Yet I'm somehow seen as over the hill and just treading water," complained a senior engineer in a large construction company.

A sixty-two-year-old secretary/administrative assistant felt that she was expected to do only "cookie-cutter" work. When she took the initiative to learn word processing on her own time, she was told, "You're not paid to have that responsibility. Just keep doing what you're doing now."

"Workers up to age 70 and often beyond can learn as well as younger workers," reports a prominent consultant. "Those who are not competent or healthy tend to drop out of the workplace. While it may take older workers somewhat longer to learn a new skill, once they get it they may be better at it than a younger worker. Also, they tend to stay on the job, as opposed to a younger worker, who may learn a new skill and then leave for a better job. Older workers also tend to have fewer accidents than younger workers because they are more careful."

Many older workers say that they are encouraged or forced to leave their jobs.

Many older workers deeply resent having their unique skills and experience devalued so that "extra bodies" can be hired. One engineer complained, "After I was encouraged to take early retirement, three workers were hired to do the work that I alone had been doing." Older workers feel that they are used to working harder and longer and with greater commitment to the organization than younger workers, but just when they are in their prime they are forced to leave. An insurance analyst said, "We know that our health benefits may cost more than a young worker's, but we feel that we've earned it. Also, is it really a saving if two or even three younger workers are hired to replace the work we did?"

Another worker who is in the personnel field disputes the extra cost of benefits. "Younger workers have dependents to be covered, which often more than makes up for extra insurance costs for an older worker. Also, recruitment and training costs are enormous for new workers."

Many older workers said that there is a perception that "we ought to be grateful that we are still on the payroll."

Many older workers say that others assume that they are weak or in poor health.

A fifty-five-year-old hospital administrator resents having people ask her if she can "make the steps" as they tour a hospital.

Younger workers often express amazement and disbelief at the amount of work that some older workers perform. "Gee, I didn't know you could still do that!" a sixty-year-old ad executive was told after working all week past 10 P.M. on a special deadline project.

As a fifty-year-old clerical worker was moving boxes, she heard one young worker say to another, "Hey, why are we letting the old lady do that?"

Many older workers say that there is too little job flexibility.

Although many older workers want to continue to work full-time, others want to work on only a part-time basis in their area of expertise. Their options, however, are usually full-time work or retirement. Part-time opportunities are usually available only for low-wage positions such as clerical workers or fast-food-restaurant employees.

Scenes from the Workplace

Lack of Autonomy and Recognition

Fred Larson, a twenty-seven-year-old credit officer, feels that he's on the fast track. He received an M.B.A. from Harvard two years ago and, after only one year in a large bank, was made a mid-manager of commercial loans. He is a confident young man who is used to making quick decisions, and he values his independence. He knows that his boss, Bob Miller, holds him in high regard, but he is increasingly annoyed by Bob's constant questioning of his decisions. "You don't tell me enough," Bob says. "Come to me before you make a major decision. I don't want you to move so fast on your own."

Fred asks, "Have I made any mistakes so far?" "No," Bob retorts, "but I feel I just need to be more informed about what you do."

"More informed!" Fred thinks. "Is he kidding? I'm the one who's kept in the dark. I'm handed all this work, and I do it, but I don't always know why. For once, I'd like to know what the big picture is around here and what the time frame is for moving ahead."

This week Fred is furious. Last week he did all the slides for a major presentation for visiting Japanese bankers and prepared a terrific report, for which Bob commended him. Nevertheless, he was told bluntly that he could not be part of the meeting. "What a bust," Fred thinks. "This is going too far. If this is what banking is like and if it's going to continue this way, I think I should move on. I've always been interested in advertising. I'll stay here until I get something better, but I sure am going to start looking around."

What Went Wrong?

1. Bob, Fred's supervisor, stressed very close supervision; this was the business style that he was used to. He was not aware that the baby-bust generation (born after 1964), more than any other group, feels oppressed or "gnawed at" by tight supervision. This group wants and expects autonomy.
2. Although Bob was insecure about Fred's independence and questioned whether he was making the right decisions, he did not set guidelines for Fred to let him know what decisions needed Bob's approval.
3. Bob did not provide a time frame, based on an assessment of Fred's work, for when Fred could move on his own.
4. He was not aware that Fred expected to be included in a meeting with senior staff. Not being intimidated by status or position, Fred felt that it was perfectly appropriate for him to meet with the Japanese bankers. Bob used his own frame of reference, which prescribed that junior staff members did not attend meetings with senior staff and important clients.

What Should Have Been Done?

1. Bob should have set a time for structured supervisory sessions in which he laid out his expectations for quantity

and quality of work and parameters for decision making. Younger workers want supervision as part of their training process but resent the assumption that they can't make any decisions, have no common sense, and therefore must come to the supervisor every minute.

2. Knowing that young workers expect to move ahead quickly, Bob should have given Fred some ideas on career opportunities at the bank.

3. Bob should have given Fred information on his projects and how they relate to the bank's larger functions and plans. In this way, he could have tuned into Fred's need for self-fulfillment and "meaningful" work and helped him feel on the inside of what's going on.

4. If Bob felt that it was totally inappropriate for Fred to attend the meeting with the Japanese bankers, he should have explained why to Fred. He also might have explored whether it was possible to change the bank's policy on having junior staff attend such meetings.

What the Supervisor Should Have Said

"Fred, you've been here for several months now, and I notice that you seem to be chafing at my need to know how you're doing in your work and the basis for your decisions. So far, your work has been excellent, but sometimes I feel that your need for more rope and my need to know are in conflict. Let's see if we can work out a style of working together that's mutually satisfactory.

"We will begin meeting every Monday morning for an hour or less to look over your week's work and to see how it fits into the bank's larger priorities. We'll assess what information you may need from me or others to move ahead and work out a review process so that I know what's been accomplished. I'd like to give you as much leeway and freedom as possible, but first I have to be comfortable with what you are actually doing. As we work together, I see your increasing independence as a goal for both of us.

"Since I know you want to move ahead, I will try to get interesting projects that might give you opportunities to learn new skills and test your mettle.

"I know that you were unhappy about not being invited to the meeting last week, especially after all the work you did for the presentation. The fact is, however, that at this bank there's a real protocol that decides who is and who is not invited to certain meetings with clients. Sometimes, it is essential that the meetings be kept very small. I do understand your feeling excluded, though, especially when you've worked so hard on a project, and I will speak to the top executives and see if we can be more flexible whenever possible. I'll get back to you on this.

"Meanwhile, let me assure you that you are very much appreciated at the bank. We value your initiative and hope that you will have a successful future with us."

Organizational Bureaucracy and Communication Style

Susan Sabatini, a twenty-five-year-old program assistant in a large nonprofit agency, was rebuked several months ago by her boss, Marlene Bryant, who accused her of having poor judgment and of not understanding organizational bureaucracy. The reason for the criticism was that Susan, who works on several international refugee projects, needed translation of several letters and went to another department in the organization for help. Since she isn't fluent in French she went to an acquaintance who did translations and asked if he would be willing to translate the documents. He willingly agreed. Somehow Susan's boss found out about this and was incensed that Susan did not come to her for help first. She felt that Susan should not have gone to another department. Marlene said, "This reflects badly on our department. If you need help on anything, come to me first."

Now, when Marlene is going over Susan's performance review, she cites this instance as an indication of Susan's lack of judgment and understanding of organizational structure. Susan reacts strongly and says, "I think it's preposterous to make such a big deal out of such a petty matter. That's so ridiculously bureaucratic. I'm a free person. I should be able to speak to anyone I want to. I certainly hope you are not going to hold this against me in getting ahead in this organization. I've already been here a year, and I feel that my job should be upgraded and that I should be given new assignments." Marlene is very annoyed and replies, "Susan, you've got a real attitude. That's the trouble with your generation. You want everything so fast. Do you know that it took me fifteen years to get to my position? Now you want to do it practically in six months. Listen, you need a lot more seasoning at what you're doing right now before you go any-where."

Susan asks what she has to do to get promoted to a higher level, and Marlene is vague, saying that she just has to wait her turn. Susan leaves the appraisal session thinking that she really has to start thinking about where else she could work that would offer a better chance for advancement and where she could work with a more "with-it" boss.

What Went Wrong?

1. Marlene apparently had never conveyed to Susan her view of organizational structure, which required all con-tacts with other departments to be cleared through her. Susan had no idea that there was anything wrong with approaching someone from another department. She sim-ply had no idea of bureaucratic lines and the implications for Marlene.
2. Marlene did not understand how casual Susan, as a younger worker, would be about organizational structure and bureaucratic lines. She thought all this "stuff" was just ridiculous. Marlene did not even consider whether Susan's point of view had any validity.
3. When Susan asked Marlene about getting ahead, she was given no encouragement or time frame whatsoever. She was left with the impression that she might have to do the same assignment for years, just because that was what Marlene had had to do.

What Should Have Been Done?

1. When Susan was hired, Marlene should have explained her expectations about working in the department and made it clear that if Susan ever had a problem in her work, she should come to Marlene before going to anyone

else, especially someone in a different department, and she would try to assist Susan.

2. Marlene should definitely consider whether her expectations of organizational structure are too rigid and whether everything should have to go through her. Such rules make the workers feel that they have very little decision-making authority, even on minor issues. The strict notion of a vertical hierarchy is fast becoming outmoded in many companies.

   If Marlene was concerned about her staff infringing on the time of other departments, she could have explained that to Susan as the reason for her concern.

3. Marlene offered Susan no help on career planning. In response to Susan's question, Marlene simply gave vent to her resentment about how long she had to work before being promoted. Marlene should have given Susan specifics on the kinds of tasks she had to master, what future opportunities she might have, and what she might have to do to qualify for promotion within the department or for another place higher in the organization.

What the Manager Might Have Said

"Susan, I appreciate your initiative in getting the documents translated, but someone in our department might have been able to do it just as easily. Please check with me first if you need some help. I know that asking someone you know to help you out with a translation doesn't seem like a big deal, but sometimes I've had flak from other supervisors when their workers are interrupted by people from other departments. Fortunately, in your case that didn't happen. If I'm not around when you need help that's not available in our own department, please make sure that you check with the person you do ask for help about his or her workload before the person helps you out. We do try to be cooperative with one another throughout the organization, but each department still sees its own work as priority."

In response to Susan's inquiries about career opportunities, Marlene might have said, "Susan, you have shown a lot of creativity and initiative on the job, and we really value that here.

There are many things connected to this job that you still haven't mastered, such as budgeting, developing new programs, and grant writing. Once you've shown that you can do these kinds of things, I will be glad to expand your functions and put you in for a raise in this job or recommend you for a job in another department."

Denied Opportunity for Training and Promotion

Midge Shanahan, age 55, has been employed at a large brokerage company for more than thirty years, working her way up from a clerical position to that of supervisor of a large clerical unit in the operations department. She is well thought of and always receives excellent evaluations. When she sees a posting for a new computer position requiring three months of training, she decides to apply. Although the position will not initially pay more than she is already earning, she feels that it has much more long-term potential for both salary and professional growth than her current job.

Midge does not get the job, but someone she supervises in her own department does—a thirty-year-old woman who had come on the job only the previous year. When Midge goes to the personnel department to ask why she was not selected, the personnel officer, Eve Bell, is evasive and implies that the worker selected has a good background and will be at the company longer than Midge, and, besides, Midge is doing such an excellent job that it would be difficult to replace her. In fact, the department head of the computer section told the personnel director that she liked Midge a great deal and seriously considered her because of her experience and reputation but was worried about whether Midge could catch on as fast as the younger person whom she did hire. The personnel officer, a young woman, is quite casual and implies that Midge is kind of foolish for wanting "to bother going through all that trouble and stress of a major training program." She ends the interview by saying, "At your age, I'd like to just rest on my laurels and take it easy."

Midge knows that the employment decision and the personnel officer's comments would almost certainly be considered age discrimination, but she is reluctant to take legal action. She knows it could take an emotional toll on her because a lawsuit could involve a long procedure, and she is worried about how it would affect her relationship with others in the company.

Although normally cheerful and enthusiastic about work, Midge becomes demoralized. She has heard talk about options for early retirement and is wondering whether she should take advantage of the pension benefits under this plan if it is offered to her. She thinks of an expression she had heard: "Some people retire and leave, and others retire and stay." She feels that she does not want to retire and leave; she has far too much energy left, and, besides, the benefits are great. She will stay, but with far less enthusiasm and commitment.

What Went Wrong?

1. If Midge has been automatically discounted for the position because of her age, this does indeed constitute grounds for a legal action. The words of the personnel officer certainly were insensitive, if not actually establishing grounds for a discrimination suit. (For example, "At your age, I would just rest on my laurels . . ." and "The worker who got the job will be here longer.") Age alone can never legally be considered a detriment for hiring someone; it's relevant only if someone is unable actually to perform the job in question (this holds true for someone younger as well).
2. Of course, there could have been some bona fide reason for hiring the younger worker based on her background; however, it is likely that Midge was not even considered because of her age.
3. Not wanting to find a replacement for Midge in her current job is not a legitimate reason for excluding Midge from consideration for a job promotion.

What Should Have Been Done?

1. The human resources department should have a clear policy, known to all supervisory and management person-

nel, on laws regarding age discrimination (as well as other discrimination). In addition to the legal issue, the department should be concerned about the maximum utilization of all workers. Midge had enormous experience in supervision and extensive knowledge of the organization. This experience and knowledge could be of great value in another department.

It is likely that Midge, if satisfied, would work for at least another fifteen years. It is less likely that she would leave the organization than a younger worker, who might well leave for a job in another company.

2. If the person interviewing Midge had concerns about her ability with computer technology, she should have asked Midge about the equipment she was already using, her motivation to learn new technology, and other questions related to the job. Usually, in situations like this, workers are simply discounted before really being considered.

What the Computer Department Head Should Have Said

"Midge, I see that you have extensive experience in the operations department and that you are familiar with some computer work—word processing and the printouts used for payroll, etc. How much have you been involved in the computer operations in your work? Do you know any software programs? Why are you motivated to learn programming? What do you offer compared to other workers?"

If Midge had had a thorough interview, with a full description of the workload, she would have either:

1. convinced the interviewer to hire her, or
2. been convinced that there were others in the organization or who had been recruited who were, in fact, more suitable for the position because of their experience or training.

What the Personnel Officer Should Have Said

"Midge, I am glad to have the chance to speak with you about your future in our company. Although you weren't selected for this round of the computer training program, I want you to know that you will be considered for any future program. In fact, I will speak to the person who does the hiring to make sure that you will not be excluded because of your present position or because of your age. We want all of our employees to grow and develop and use the experience they have in new and diverse ways. Your many years with the company can certainly be useful in a computer department as they are in the department where you work now."

The "Pushed-Aside" Older Worker

George Greene, age 58, is a senior project director of a large architectural firm. With more than twenty-five years' experience with the company, George is highly respected for his vast technical expertise and his methodical supervision of all aspects of his construction projects. In the industry, he is considered the definitive gentleman because of his low-key approach and his courtly manners. His authority is rarely questioned.

Then things change. Walter Leahy, one of the firm's partners, hires Jim Montague, a thirty-seven-year-old project director from a competing firm, without consulting George and places him on George's project. After an initial meeting, George thinks that Jim could be an asset because he seems to know the political ropes. Jim seems to have special skills in coordinating with many departments within his former firm, as well as with city agencies. On the other hand, Jim shows a startling lack of interest in the technical aspects of the major projects George is working on.

At a staff meeting, George thinks Jim is blatantly rude. Jim interrupts George and suggests that he "move the meeting along." Jim also says, "Some of these details are trivial; let's think about the big picture." He also makes remarks implying that George is hovering over the staff, is too negative, and worries too much about potential pitfalls of the project. Jim says, "I thought we have a schedule to complete. Let's get on with it and not anticipate trouble."

Later that day, George has lunch with Walter, a partner in the firm. George says, "Jim is getting to me. That kid has no idea of what's involved in some of these projects. He promises everyone the world with no care as to whether we can deliver." Walter looks grave. "George, I'm glad you brought up the subject of Jim. On one of the next projects, I'm going to try Jim as the manager. It's time we move some young blood up the ladder, and you've got to admit that Jim gets along very well with those younger guys out there. We've got to think of the future of the organization, develop new leadership. Besides, aren't you tired of knocking yourself out? It's time to be a technical resource for the firm, and you're the greatest in that area. Let the young ones move it along."

George makes an excuse and leaves lunch abruptly. "This is what loyalty to one's firm comes to? Twenty-five years and I'm pushed aside? We're in a recession. Will I be next to go? Is it my age? My management style? Is this the way my career at the firm is going to end?"

What Went Wrong?

1. Walter, the senior partner, hired Jim without George's input or consent. Although there had been some precedent for partners hiring staff without clearance from department heads, the effect of this policy was to diminish George's authority over his employee.
2. George's expertise and his contribution to the firm over the preceding twenty-five years were not acknowledged by Walter. Although Jim has special talents that the firm wants, George, too, has unique skills and experience that are invaluable, including years of experience in all aspects of very complicated construction processes and a commitment to service to the firm.
3. Walter ignored George's concerns about Jim's style, which was a source of conflict for George. Walter and George should have discussed candidly the difference between the younger and the older managers' values: George's need for caution and attention to detail and Jim's need for accommodating others' schedules and moving ahead at a brisk pace.
4. Walter did not give feedback to George on some of his deficits in management style. The firm was now stressing

greater coordination between departments within the firm and with city agencies and faster project closings. George's emphasis was on clear lines of authority, caution, and strict adherence to technical details. By not encouraging George to change, Walter was unconsciously reinforcing the stereotype about older workers' inability to adapt to changing circumstances.

5. Walter stated that George would be better off as a technical resource and should let younger people prepare for leadership, as if George could no longer be a leader. When he asked George, "Aren't you tired of knocking yourself out?" he implied that George lacked energy or ambition. The implication of Walter's remarks to George was that he was through at the firm in any leadership capacity.

What Should Have Been Done?

1. Walter should have met with George periodically to discuss his performance and to outline further expectations on both sides. Too often, experienced professionals are taken for granted and are not given feedback because it seems inappropriate at their level. But older professionals as well as younger ones need feedback and guidance on changing expectations of management in order to meet new priorities.

2. George should have been included in Walter's decision to hire Jim and place him under George's tutelage. There should have been some understanding with George that Jim was a potential project manager for additional work that would come into the firm and that he was not a replacement for George.

3. It should have been made clear to Jim that George was his superior. While Jim's ideas were welcome, George had final authority and Walter would be expected to back him up.

4. George needed feedback on his negative attitude toward younger employees. When George referred to his subordinates as "kids," this seemed to reflect his attitude that younger employees know less and need constant atten-

tion and supervision and that issues are not to be questioned or negotiated with George. George should have been told that his management style should reflect human relations skills and a team approach, not only because it is more effective within the team but also because this style is needed to coordinate among so many departments and outside agencies.

What the Partner Should Have Said to George before Hiring Jim

"George, I've just learned that Jim Montague is eager to leave his firm and wants to join us. I think this will be a great opportunity to bring new blood into the organization. Jim's got fantastic contacts, new visions, and a certain political savvy. I'd like you to supervise him because he can learn a lot from you in technical skills and overall supervision of projects. I think he will bring new clients to us and additional work that, eventually, he can direct. I'm eager to know your opinion of him, because there is no one else's judgment I respect, George, as much as yours."

What Walter Should Have Said after Hearing about the Conflict between George and Jim

"George, I'm sorry to hear about some of these conflict issues. Jim has his brash streak and maybe moves ahead more quickly than our firm has been used to. But that's one of the reasons I wanted him here. As I told you when we hired him, we anticipated using him for one or more of the new projects that he initiates for the firm. Let me assure you that this in no way diminishes our respect for your work. We expect no changes in the staffing of your projects. I have high hopes for the tremendous strengths you both bring to the firm. There's plenty of room for both of you here."

Summary

Younger and older workers face unique workplace problems. For younger workers, the issues are bureaucratic restrictions, the perceived lack of autonomy, and the lack of opportunity for timely advancement. Older workers face two typical stereotypes: their supposed inability to learn new skills and the notion that older workers are rigid and should be replaced by more flexible, younger workers.

Chapter 9
Gays and Lesbians

It is almost impossible to estimate the number of gays and lesbians in the United States, or in the workforce, because of the lack of substantive research and the reluctance of so many to be counted. A figure of 10 percent is often cited on the basis of the classic 1948 Kinsey report and other studies, but two later studies indicated a far smaller number. One study, done by the National Opinion Research Center at the University of Chicago, reported that 2.5 percent of women are lesbian and 2.8 percent of men are gay, and another study found only one percent of men gay.[1] However, gay rights activists, as well as some other researchers, question the methodology of these and other studies that show less than 10 percent of the population to be gay or lesbian.

The lack of accurate numbers on the size of the gay and lesbian population points out a salient issue: fear of disclosure because of concerns about discrimination and social censure or exclusion.

There is no federal law prohibiting discrimination based on sexual orientation. Title VII of the Civil Rights Act of 1964 does not include sexual orientation as a protected classification. Employment protection for gays and lesbians resides in the laws of eight states and the District of Columbia, in more than one hundred municipal laws, and in the management policies of a small number of private corporations. In all, it is estimated that about one third of all workers in the United States are covered by some kind of law or policy prohibiting discrimination against gays and lesbians, and these vary widely in their provisions.

Moreover, there is an effort by some groups to prevent or overturn municipal laws that provide protection against discrimination based on sexual orientation. In 1992, voters in Colorado approved an amendment to the state constitution prohibiting legislation protecting gays and lesbians. Although a lower level state court ruled the amendment unconstitutional, the state has appealed the ruling to the highest court of Colorado. It is possible that the case will eventually be decided by the U.S. Supreme Court.

Because of social disapproval and the lack of protective legislation, most gays and lesbians choose not to "come out" in the workplace. Most anticipate outright discrimination in employment decisions of hiring and promotion and a workplace norm of homophobic jokes and overt hostility. They also recognize the reality that few openly gay workers have visible leadership positions in the corporate world. The issue of AIDS has exacerbated discrimination against gay men because of fear and misinformation about the disease and its spread.

For those who have come out, other employment issues include a desire for social acceptance of their sexual orientation and the extension of employee benefits to domestic partners.

Because acceptance of gays and lesbians may touch on religious issues and may call into question and threaten basic assumptions about gender identity, for many heterosexuals there is a collective denial and a wall of secrecy about gays and lesbians in the workplace.

Voices of Gays and Lesbians in the Workplace

Most gays and lesbians say that because of their invisibility, others they work with don't even realize their existence.

A hospital administrator who is a lesbian said, "I can sum up the work issue for gays and lesbians in two words: 'WE HIDE.' " A male accountant said, "We are mostly in the closet—especially in the professions."

Although more gays and lesbians are coming out, most feel it is necessary to hide their sexual orientation—to be invisible—to avoid the risk of losing their jobs or of being harassed or rejected by fellow workers.

Over and over again gays and lesbians used the words *invisibility* and *closeted* to describe their status. A product development manager said, "We are the invisible minority. Yes, some celebrities, government officials, and gay-rights advocates are 'out,' i.e., open about their sexual orientation, but not your average, run-of-the-mill person working in a homophobic organization." A gay operations supervisor said, "It is easy to be invisible. Contrary to what most straight people think, there is usually no way to tell from appearances that we are gay or lesbian. Most of us look exactly like everyone else. It is only a small percentage who are flamboyantly or noticeably gay or lesbian and easily identified."

"Although many straight people say they don't know anyone who is gay or lesbian, they do—they just don't know that they do," said a gay engineer at a manufacturing company.

Most gays and lesbians say that most nongays don't realize that there is no federal legal protection against discrimination based on sexual orientation.

Although many people think that gays and lesbians are covered by civil rights legislation, federal laws do not provide protection against discrimination based on sexual orientation. A systems analyst said, "Many people think we are pressing for special rights, but all we want is what other groups have that have experienced discrimination." Another worker added, "Holding a job is not a special right—it is basic to survival, and our sexual orientation shouldn't be held against us."

Gays and lesbians say that others don't realize the extent of discrimination they experience in the workplace.

An insurance claims agent said, "We all know that there are ghettos in American industry where it is acceptable for known gays and lesbians to work—mainly it's on lower levels and in the back rooms." Although the stereotype is that most gay men are in the arts or in fashion, the reality is that most are in computer technology or the health care industry. According to a study cited in *Fortune* magazine, "Forty percent more gays are employed in finance and insurance than in entertainment and the arts; and ten times as many work in computers as in fashion."[2]

A computer specialist who has worked for large law firms and investment houses said, "You can get to the top in some areas—*behind the scenes*—but in senior management or jobs involving the public, forget it!"

A lesbian mortgage broker said, "I was on the fast track in my company—I was on special committees, getting bonuses, the whole works. Somehow my employer found out that I had a female domestic partner and—pow—it took no time before I was fired. Despite my not being out and being considered an attractive woman, the mere fact of my being a lesbian was enough to get me fired. There was no law to protect me from this. I found out from others that my boss automatically assumed I was an immoral person, committing an act against God because of my sexual orientation."

Many reasons are given for discrimination against known gays and lesbians, from "What will the customers think?" to a personal abhorrence or discomfort.

It is a widespread concern among gays and lesbians that hiring and promotional opportunities for them are definitely limited once they come out. Some gay men say the discrimination is not just related to hiring and promotion and that they are subjected to ridicule and violence. A mailroom supervisor known by his fellow workers to be gay said that obscene graffiti about him were written in restrooms and on walls. When he complained to his supervisors, little was done. One supervisor tried to intervene and was told by the boss to "forget about it" and let the worker deal with it himself. Other gay men have said that when someone comes to their defense in a hostile situation, that person is often called "fag" or "faggot-lover" by other workers. A retired fireman said, "Violent gay-bashing does not take place just on the streets. It's a workplace phenomenon, too. Look at the recent case of the sailor in the U.S. Navy who was killed by his shipmate because he was gay."

Some gays and lesbians say they are penalized for their failure to conform to heterosexual gender roles.

For someone open about his or her sexual orientation, there are penalties apart from being fired. A male secretary was told to "tone down" his behavior when he brought in flowers and cookies to his male boss. His supervisor said, "We don't like the way you move, either. Can't you wear your clothes looser and walk straight?" "In other words, I had to look and act like my supervisor or I was reprimanded, even though my work was known to be excellent," the secretary said.

This man, and others, feels that there should be an acceptance of open differences in behavior or style for gays and lesbians, just as there may be for ethnic or racial groups. "While it's true that most gays and lesbians act the same as anyone who is straight, there are those of us who do act in a different way. Can't that be accepted?"

Although some gays and lesbians feel that dress and styles of behavior should not be dictated by management, others feel that *everyone* has to know what's appropriate behavior in his or her own organization and that it's important to fit into the norm to get ahead. The issue is how narrow the norm should be.

Gays and lesbians say that some coworkers and supervisors are extremely uncomfortable dealing with them and even with the topic of sexual orientation.

A lesbian magazine writer said, "Some people do know I'm a lesbian because of the picture of my lover in my office and because I bring her to occasional office events, but whenever I talk about my sexual orientation or my partner, people usually act embarrassed. Many people fumble when they even say the word *lesbian* or *gay man*. They just can't even get the words out of their mouths." A gay telecommunication specialist said, "It would kill my boss to even say the words *sexual orientation*. It's like there's a horrible taboo about the topic."

Gays and lesbians say that others don't realize the range of diversity within their ranks.

A gay environmental lawyer said, "I know gay Republicans, Democrats, grandparents, artists, bankers. Within any group of gays and lesbians, there will be the usual range of personality types, races, religions, professions, and interests. Being gay is just one part of our lives."

A television writer who is gay said, "The media really perpetuate the stereotypes of who gays and lesbians are—they always seem to show the extreme elements of our community."

Gays and lesbians say that it is unfair that their long-term partners are denied benefits, primarily health benefits, that are provided to spouses of heterosexual workers.

"Most benefits were devised to protect families," said a laboratory technician who is a lesbian. Originally benefits were provided for the female spouses of straight men and for their children. As women entered the workforce, their husbands were also included in benefits packages. But the family constellation has changed. Only 24 percent of all households consist of a married man and woman with children. A gay legal librarian queried, "What about benefits for all the rest?"

The major benefit discussed is health benefits. Although most organizations do *not* provide benefits to same-sex partners, there are a growing number of companies that are making these provisions. A gay human resources manager said, "Ironically, once a company makes a policy providing benefits for gay and lesbian partners, few people take advantage. Perhaps, it's because so many of us are still not out."

Gays and lesbians say that some others assume that sexual orientation is a life choice or preference, which in most cases is not true.

A gay systems engineer said, "We don't like the terms *sexual preference* and *life-style* because they connote choice—and we are not choosing. I feel that we are biologically wired in a different way from nongays. Most of us feel we have always been different, even those who come to the full recognition later in life. That's why we like the term *sexual orientation* to describe our life-style."

Other gays and lesbians in the workplace report that when their life-style is viewed in terms of orientation and not choice, there is more acceptance from coworkers and supervisors.

All gays and lesbians say they are offended by stereotypical jokes and demeaning terms used about them in the workplace.

"I deeply resent jokes about 'faggots,' " said a gay magazine editor. "Queen, butch, dyke—these are all vile terms and gay-baiting." A lesbian personnel official said that the latest jokes—particularly vicious ones—are about AIDS and gays. "AIDS jokes are all over the place, and I work in a highly professional company that prides itself on its liberal gay-rights policy."

Many gays and lesbians say that to come out is to lose their credibility at work.

A financial adviser's sexual orientation became known after he was on his job in an investment firm for five years. He said, "As soon as my colleagues found out I was gay, everything changed. I was avoided, almost shunned. I wasn't invited to meetings with other corporations, and one of my clients was assigned to someone else."

Other gays and lesbians say that when they come out, other workers' perceptions of them seem to change dramatically. A chemist said, "All of a sudden, we're not seen as fully professional but as morally deficient in character. Our loyalty is in question; we are no longer to be trusted. It's as if we are going to steal or trade secrets with another company." A salesman said, "I'm the same person with the same skills and talents, but now I'm seen as something abnormal or as a person with a mental illness. The bottom line is that I'm not as trusted or valued as I was before."

A lesbian office manager came out to her company after working there for twenty years. Her boss and several other senior managers belong to a conservative religious group. She said, "I feel that I am now perceived as being immoral and evil and as living an unnatural way of life. They didn't fire me because I've been here so long, but I didn't get the promotion a few months ago that I clearly deserved. They're keeping me on, probably hoping to 'educate' me. If I thought I could get another job, I definitely wouldn't stay here."

Many gays and lesbians say they are viewed by some only in terms of their sex life.

A lesbian programmer who is an open member of a gay and lesbian caucus group at work said, "Why am I defined only by my sexual orientation? All everyone sees is the sex thing." A gay accounts manager said, "There are no beds in the office. There are desks, chairs, and computers. But I feel that some people seem to define me solely by my sexual orientation and not by my professional capabilities."

Gay men say that many workers assume that all gays have or will have the HIV virus or AIDS and that the disease can be transmitted by casual contact in the workplace.

"Despite the information campaigns and the data, many people can't get it into their heads that not all gay men have AIDS and that heterosexuals can have it, too," said a public relations specialist.

"I see the fear and tentativeness of some coworkers when they're told I'm gay," said a training director. He described visiting another department and asking for a cup of coffee. There were at least five mugs on the shelf in the coffee area used by staff. "But a staff member went crazy looking all over for a paper cup. I ended the whole embarrassing scene by saying, 'Never mind, I drink too much coffee anyway.' But I was furious, not only because of the inference that I had the virus, but also because people assumed it would be transmitted by sharing the same cup."

Many gays and lesbians who are not out say they spend so much energy hiding their sexual orientation that it detracts from their productivity.

"I'm not myself. I'm uncomfortable. There is this wall of secrecy that affects everything at work," said an actuarial assistant. "I'm afraid my lover will call; I'm afraid people might see my friends," said a magazine editor. Another lesbian, a secretary, added, "I'm so tired of being vague about what I did last weekend or why I don't want to be fixed up on a date." A gay marketing manager said, "I avoid all conversation of a personal nature. It's so hard to have two lives; it drains me. Too much of my energy that should go into work goes into this pretense."

A gay divisional sales manager said, "There's a tremendous amount of socializing in my business, and I either go to functions alone or have a woman friend as my 'date.' I feel like a real fraud, but I feel that's the only way I can stay in this job. It's very stressful."

Some gays and lesbians in the workforce say they are offended by coworkers' inappropriate questions about their sexual orientation.

"If you are out in the workplace, some coworkers feel free to ask you very personal questions," said a project manager. She added, "I don't mind if someone expresses a genuine interest in my life, but what I strongly object to are prurient questions about my sexual practices or questions that try to educate me out of my 'life-style.' A few people have actually said, 'What do lesbians actually do together?' or 'Do you think you'd feel differently toward men if you met a really nice, sensitive guy?' or 'Don't you think you're upsetting your parents?' "

A gay insurance manager said, "I would like people to talk about my social life in the same way they discuss their own— where did you go on vacation; what did you do on the weekends? I want people to know that my life partner means as much to me as someone in a heterosexual marriage. I want to be considered a normal person."

Scenes from the Workplace

"Hiding" and Its Costs

Gail Lewis has recently been promoted to a position as associate manager of public relations in a cosmetic company, a position she has held for the past four months. She keeps her identity as a lesbian hidden.

Although her company has a strong policy statement prohibiting discrimination based on sexual orientation, Gail knows that the policy is, in reality, enforced at the discretion of individual managers. In some units it is acceptable to be out, whereas in others being out means limited opportunities if not actual dismissal on some pretext. Few people have filed discrimination complaints because they don't want the publicity, which they feel will follow them throughout their career.

Gail is not sure about the stance of her manager, Ellen Barbieri. Although Ellen is very friendly and supportive of Gail in her work, Ellen has never made reference to the gay-rights policy at staff meetings. In several instances concerning social events in the department, she has told staff that they are free to bring their husbands, wives, girlfriends, or boyfriends. Ellen clearly assumes that everyone is heterosexual.

At meetings and social functions attended by both Gail

and Ellen, antigay jokes are told, and Ellen makes no negative comment in response and occasionally even smiles.

Faking or hiding has always been difficult for Gail. With the new position, her stress is heightened because of the numerous social situations that are part of her job. Gail spends a considerable amount of time with Ellen at these functions and is constantly fabricating stories about her social life and making excuses for her unwillingness to be "fixed up." She is very uncomfortable discussing her personal life and occasionally is inconsistent with the names, places, and events of her social life. In one instance Ellen commented, "I thought you said your date for the opera was Pete, not Jim." Gail explained this contradiction away but was worried that a similar slipup could happen again and make Ellen suspect her sexual orientation.

Recently Gail was invited to speak at an interdepartmental meeting. Although she is an experienced speaker, she panicked and canceled her presentation. She feels that she is a sham, that no one really knows who she is. She notices that her writing seems more constricted and she feels that hiding affects every aspect of her work, that all her energies are sapped by her double life. Yet she is afraid that if she comes out, her credibility and even her position will be in jeopardy.

What Went Wrong?

1. Ellen, the manager, did not make clear her support for the company's antidiscrimination policy, which covers gays and lesbians.
2. Ellen's language did not encompass gays and lesbians. Ellen assumed everyone is heterosexual. She did not seem to be aware of the fact that many gays and lesbians hide their sexual orientation at work.
3. Ellen did not notice Gail's discomfort when talking about her personal life.
4. Ellen was not a model of managerial responsibility when she listened to antigay jokes without expressing her disapproval.

What Should Have Been Done?

1. At appropriate times during staff meetings, Ellen should
   have mentioned the company's antidiscrimination policy
   and stated that she strongly supports the policy and
   expects all staff members to do so as well. She could have
   added that the company is supportive of all workers,
   regardless of race, ethnicity, gender, disability, or sexual
   orientation; what matters is the effectiveness of their
   work.
2. Ellen's language should have been inclusive of different
   sexual orientations and should not have implied that
   everyone is heterosexual. Instead of "husband, wife, girl-
   friend, or boyfriend," she might have said "significant
   other" or "life partner." She should try to be comfortable
   using the terms *gay, lesbian,* and *sexual orientation.*
3. When Ellen heard the antigay jokes, she should have
   indicated that she thought the jokes reinforced stereotypes about gays and that they could be hurtful to any
   gays in the organization who might hear the jokes.

What Ellen Might Have Said

"Gail, I'm concerned that you seem to be pretty stressed out
lately. I know you had to cancel your presentation and that you
seem very uncomfortable at some of the social gatherings we've
had. Is it because you're feeling shy in the new job, or is it
anything else that I can help you with? You know I think highly
of your skills—that's why we promoted you—and I'd like to be
as helpful as I can."

If Gail denies there is a problem, Ellen could either drop the
conversation or add, "Well, if there ever is a problem, please feel
free to come to me if I can help. I value you both professionally
and personally."

If during their continued friendly working relationship, Gail
tells Ellen that she is a lesbian, Ellen might say, "I am really glad
that you told me so that we can be open with each other. You've
already heard me speak at meetings of my strong support for
our company's antidiscrimination policy protecting everyone,

including gays and lesbians. I also want to support you in your decision if you want to come out to others in the department. But that's up to you. In any case, let me assure you that coming out will have no adverse effect on your career goals in this department, as far as I'm concerned."

Resistance to Gays in High-Exposure Jobs

Ray Sherman, known at his company to be gay, is the assistant director of sales for a large flooring company. The company has no policy statement concerning sexual orientation and is in a state and a city that have no gay rights legislation. However, Ray's sexual orientation has never been an issue at the company. Ray rarely talks to his associates about his personal life, but he does not hide the fact that he has lived with the same man for the past twenty years and that he is an active volunteer at the Gay Men's Health Clinic.

Ray is a highly valued and respected employee of the company, where he has worked for the past fifteen years. He has also held several positions in flooring industry associations. When his company's director of regional sales announces that he is retiring, Ray applies for the job.

At the promotion interview, the company directors are cordial but blunt. "I don't know anyone who is more qualified for this job than you, Ray," says the regional director of operations, "but we have a real concern. Your life-style is your business, but I don't know how it will be received in your new high-exposure position, particularly in this conservative region of the country. I don't know if the company can risk the negative attitudes that may come up and that will affect your ability to do your job. I'm not sure that we're ready yet to go with this promotion. We'll have to give it more thought." The other directors nod in agreement.

Two weeks later, Ray is told that the position has been given to the director of sales of a competing flooring company, who has far less experience than Ray. Ray is extremely disappointed and demoralized but not surprised.

What Went Wrong?

1. The company had no policy against discrimination based on sexual orientation.

2. Although the company valued Ray as an outstanding employee, it automatically assumed that his promotion to a more highly visible job would result in customer resistance and have a negative effect on the company.

What Should Have Been Done?

1. The company should have had an antidiscrimination policy that covered sexual orientation.
2. The company should have realized that if the best person for the job happened to be gay, that person's talent should not be wasted.
3. Although Ray's visibility might have affected his customers, it is more likely that familiarity with Ray would have led to his acceptance by business contacts.
4. The company should have selected Ray for the job, introduced him to key customers with the company's full support, and treated the promotion like any other business decision.

What the Regional Director Might Have Said

"Ray, we're pleased to offer you this promotion. If your past performance is any indication, you should be top-notch in the job. We'll be meeting at the flooring convention next week, and we will announce your promotion then. Also, we're going to arrange some dinner meetings with top customers to make the transition easier. We don't anticipate any problems on the so-called life-style issue, but if there are, let us know. You have our full commitment and support."

Summary

The basic workplace issue for gays and lesbians is the threat of outright discrimination and ostracism because of their sexual orientation. That threat forces most lesbians and gays to remain hidden, resulting in stress and lowered productivity. For those who are out, visible high-level positions are virtually unattainable in many organizations.

Chapter 10
Women

In 1990 women represented 45.4 percent of the workforce, and it is anticipated that by 2000 that number will increase to 50 percent.[1]

The labor force is still segregated, with more than 94 percent of all secretarial, nursing, and child-care jobs held by women. Nevertheless, women are increasingly moving into nontraditional, professional, and managerial positions.

Forty-three percent of first-line supervisors and middle managers are now women. But it is at the next higher level that women feel the brunt of discrimination most heavily. Only 3 percent of corporate executives are women, and of the four thousand highest paid executives in the country, only 0.5 percent are women.

Furthermore, despite the Equal Pay Act of 1963, in 1990 women earned only seventy-four cents for every dollar earned by a man. Even taking into account differences in education and experience in the work world, the pay gap is real. At every age, within every work category, men still take home more pay than women. And the more education a woman has, the wider the gap.

In addition to the fact that women earn less, have less prestigious job titles, and are promoted less often, many women face the reality of problematic child care, which can have a detrimental effect on job opportunities. Many women are worried that only childless women can really make it in the corporate world. Corporations are now looking hard at how to meet the challenges of parental leave, flex-time, and child-care assistance. There is an urgency about providing adequate child-care arrangements since, by 1995, two thirds of all preschool children, or approximately 15 million children, and more than three quarters of all school-age children will have mothers in the workforce.[2]

There are more subtle issues, too: the perception that a woman's style of leadership is different from—and less effective than—a man's, the persistent cultural norm that women should be in subordinate roles, and the perception that women are less competent than men.

Women of color and other minorities, immigrant women, women with disabilities, and lesbians face additional problems. The issues described in this chapter, however, apply to all women in the workplace. Despite federal legislation passed during the past thirty years to deal with the issues of discrimination in hiring and promotion and of sexual harassment, discrimination against women in the workplace still remains.

Voices of Women in the Workplace

Many women say that no matter how hard they work, how much education they have, and what their title or responsibility, they still make less money than men with the equivalent education and experience.

"We all know the statistics; in 1990 the Labor Department reported that women make seventy-four cents for every dollar males make. We're the bargains of the work world," said one woman director of marketing.

"So what did the Equal Pay Act do for us?" asked a woman account executive. "It's thirty years later, and the optimists are saying, 'Well, it's better than the sixty cents to the dollar that we made in the sixties and seventies.' Maybe that's true, maybe we can now be partners in law firms, corporate vice presidents, and senior engineers, but even then our authority and status—and pay—often don't match men's." A senior financial analyst at a large brokerage firm said, "We're not getting men's salaries. I know for a fact that a man in my job would be making at least $20,000 more a year. Men usually get paid more for the same job than women—experience and education being the same—that's known by all the women."

Many women say they are excluded, directly or indirectly, from the informal men's network.

A woman banking manager said, "Before and after most meetings, especially important ones, there's all this informal bunching in twos or threes of men talking together. When I try to be included, I'm made to feel I'm crashing a party to which I wasn't invited! I know they're sharing important information or planning strategy—crucial stuff—and I'm not privy to it."

As an example, a woman production manager recalled that she was standing with three men in her department after a meeting and they started planning departmental strategy and politics. Suddenly, one of the men turned to her and said, "You don't have to stay now. Why don't you go upstairs? I'll see you later." While he was saying this, he made several gestures with his hand to shoo her away dismissively. She stayed, but she sensed that the intensity of the conversation stopped, and she felt that the "real stuff" would be discussed among the men later.

Another woman executive said that when she is at an off-site training program or convention, the men group around the bar, drinking, talking about sports, and telling off-color jokes, or else they're off playing poker. "The guys in my department seem to bond at bars, restaurants with belly dancers, or the golf course. Where does that leave me and the other women?"

Many women, especially those who have been successful, say that they spend a tremendous amount of energy trying to enter the "boys' club" or the "old boys' network"—"the male bonding thing." "I often wonder if it's worth all the effort. I would like once to be invited by them instead of always inviting myself to places I don't particularly even want to go," said one.

A senior manager said sadly, "There's such a sense of loneliness in being excluded from the power structure and even from the informal gatherings. It's true we form our own, but our networks are still seen as secondary and don't really have the same power."

Many women say that men do not listen to them when they speak, whether in meetings or on a one-to-one basis.

A product development manager said, "I can't tell you how many times I have made suggestions in meetings that were totally ignored." A banking official said, "Just last week, I was reporting on my task-force findings, when I was interrupted by one of the men, who then changed the topic and deflected the conversation to the other men in the room. When I said I wanted to finish my report, I was accused of being uptight and rigid for sticking so narrowly to the agenda. The men attacked me as if I was doing something wrong, when it was the guy who stepped over me and ignored my presentation."

A human resources manager said that either she is not heard—making her feel ignored and invisible—or her ideas are stolen by one of the men or shot down as unworthy. "They're called unworkable, not researched enough, done before, too complicated, too simplistic, too expensive. The bottom line is, 'Your idea is no good.' "

Many women say that pregnancy and childbirth often result in the loss or downgrading of their jobs.

A sales executive said, "As soon as I told men I was pregnant, there was a total reversal in how they reacted to me. From being a committed professional, I was seen as somehow a half-baked worker." She continued, "Suddenly, territories were shifted away from me; new staff I was supposed to hire were cut from my budget. I knew I was somehow diminished as a serious professional in the men's eyes."

Many women confirm that pregnancy and childbirth often restrict women's professional status and opportunities, even when the women do not wish to change their professional lives and have made all the needed arrangements to handle child care and work. Deborah Swiss and Judith Walker, in a new study, call this the "maternal wall."[3]

"Many men simply do not believe that women can have both a career and a family," a woman attorney said emphatically. An insurance clerk said, "Every stereotype you can imagine gets thrown up at us: 'You won't be as reliable—you'll be staying out whenever your kid is sick,' 'You won't be as committed to the job; you'll always want to leave early,' 'Pregnant women do not come back to work—I had two women work here who didn't.' "

A woman account executive said, "Maybe it's because most men still don't really worry about family obligations; their focus is only on their jobs. So they wonder how we can do both. Yes, having children is another consideration, but we want to do both and can. Sometimes, there may be accommodations needed, but aren't families everyone's responsibility?"

A woman economist said, "Let's get some reality in here. Seventy-four percent of women with children from six to eighteen and 52 percent of women with children under two are in the workforce—and somehow manage to do their work and be mothers, too."

An associate at a large law firm says that she is undercut by being called "mommy" in totally inappropriate ways. If she has to go out of town on business, colleagues will say, "How's Mommy going to take care of the little kiddies?"; if she makes a suggestion to a peer, he might say, "Stop mommying me; this isn't your home."

Many women say that there is no flexibility about work hours, making it hard for them to both perform at a high level of effectiveness and meet their family responsibilities.

A manufacturer's sales representative said, "If I could work part-time or have flexible hours, I would be much more likely to stay here. Friends of mine who are really satisfied work at firms where there is flexibility of scheduling, facilities for child care on-site, and extended leaves of absence after childbirth. Some places even let you work part-time or full-time at home." A female office worker said, "I was thinking of leaving my company, and they've come up with a great new idea that has made me stay— emergency care. This means if my babysitter arrangements fall through at the last minute, I can take my kids to work. It's only for twenty days a year, but just knowing there is this backup is a tremendous relief." Yet such arrangements are rare.

Many women say that sexual harassment is prevalent in the workplace and that it's all about power.

"It's not really the quid-pro-quo variety—'put-out-or-get-out' harassment—that's most prevalent," said a woman accountant. "It's sexual harassment in terms of creating a hostile and demeaning environment." "I resent having my anatomy discussed in front of clients," a woman systems analyst said. "I'm furious at the men who toss condoms to each other in front of me and who have computer graphics of naked women," said a computer programmer. "When men make off-color remarks or tell bawdy jokes at meetings, I think it's meant to put me in my place. The comments about 'how great your blouse shows your figure off' are meant to remind me and others of our sexual difference, which has always meant male dominance and female subservience." A woman engineer reiterated this point: "It's not about flirtatiousness or even about sex. It's about humiliation of women and intimidation and resentment because we are moving into a formerly male world. The purpose is to undercut our professionalism and credibility."

Many women say that to complain about offensive sexual behavior in the workplace is to be blamed.

"If we complain about the hostile atmosphere at work, which is sexually charged and offensive, it's implied that we somehow brought it on ourselves by our clothes or behavior. Or we're told that we're exaggerating or that we should learn to get along with difficult people—that this is an isolated situation. Men have no idea what it does to my self-confidence when everything is made into a sexual reference," said a woman assistant vice president of a bank.

To add insult to injury, many women say that they are accused of being humorless and prudes or "prunes" when they don't laugh at sexual jokes. A woman computer analyst was told, "Lighten up; if you want to play with the big boys, you've got to take the heat."

Many women say there is a huge discrepancy in how men and women perceive justice in sexual harassment cases.

"How can I complain about my boss who is always brushing up against me 'accidentally' and who, at out-of-town conferences, appears at my hotel room door at midnight to ask me if I have the *New York Times*?" said an administrative assistant. "Who are they going to believe?" "We all know women are forced out, and men remain in power. To file a complaint is career suicide," said an associate in a large law firm.

Indeed, statistics bear out this perception. A 1990 *Working Women* survey found that 55 percent of the women who reported harassment learned that nothing happened to the accused man, while only 17 percent of the women suffered no ill effects to their own careers.⁴ As an example of why women often don't even bother to file a complaint, a newspaper writer said, "With all this, we continue to work for men who harass us, because we need the job."

Many women say that men assume that they have advanced in their careers by using their sexuality.

A thirty-five-year-old executive is asked, "So who did you sleep with to get where you are?" A senior account executive at a large advertising company was able to obtain a major new client. After she was seen lunching with an executive from the new client organization, one of her male peers said, "Oh, I saw you had a hot date with your new account—you really know how to flirt your way into a great contract."

Women say that some men assume that in order for a woman to get a promotion or obtain a client, there must be a romantic relationship or at least an unfair use of flirting and sex appeal. A woman quality-assurance manager said, "If we get ahead, men seem to think it's either because of affirmative action or sex. What about competence, expertise, hard work—why aren't those mentioned?"

Many women say that some men have a hard time being supervised by women because they are used to having men in charge and wielding authority.

"Taking orders from a woman triggers the feelings they had when they were children and dominated by their mothers or schoolteachers. It makes them feel like little boys. Once they're men, they need to be in control, but they can accept orders from other men. It's almost a kind of primitive feeling," said a woman hospital administrator.

A woman sales representative said, "One guy actually said to me, 'Men are supposed to rule the universe! Isn't God a man?' I know that was pretty crude and most guys wouldn't say it so bluntly, but I have the feeling that many men really believe that in their guts."

Many women say they're in a no-win situation when it comes to management style.

"I'm damned if I do and damned if I don't," said a director of communications. "If I'm direct and independent, I'm called a tough bitch. And yet when men exhibit the same behavior, it's fine. They're called forceful. On the other hand, if I try a conciliatory, cooperative approach, I'm considered a wimp or a 'mommy.' "

Some women report that they play the tentative-sounding woman in order to be more likable and accepted. "It's hard to strike the right note," said a woman planning director. "To be respected and believed, we have to be very direct and assertive; yet when we do this, we are often called unfeminine, castrating, or worse." Sometimes men are demeaning. A bank loan officer reported that after she had a strong disagreement with a male colleague about a major loan application, he said to her, "What's the matter—you must have PMS or be 'on the rag'—you're not thinking straight." She added, "Of course, he didn't have the facts to back up his position on the loan. He just couldn't take my coming on strong."

Finding the right management style has been difficult for some women, but others see their managerial positions as offering an opportunity for a much-needed leadership change. "I'm not going to use a carbon copy of men's dictatorial, controlling style that says 'win, win, win, kill, kill, kill,' " said a tax specialist at a large management consulting firm.

A woman insurance manager said, "The so-called female management style that is personal, motivating, interactive, and accessible is working. Creativity and productivity are the issues, and you don't get them with the typical style of male leadership that is hierarchical and militaristic. Men see themselves as the boss, the power, while we see ourselves as motivators and empowerers of the entire workforce. And that's the style of the future."

Many women say that at meetings, secretarial tasks are often handed to them by male peers and bosses.

A senior investment analyst said, "It is assumed that a woman will serve as the support person, even though our titles and positions are the same as the men's. When I refused to be the note taker, the men gave me withering looks and one muttered to another, 'What a defensive broad.' Despite my Ph.D. in finance, it's somehow assumed that I'm there to 'carry the pencils' to the meetings."

Many women say that they are viewed as too emotional and that men confuse emotional expressiveness with weakness.

"Men think they can't give us feedback, that we'll break down, that we can't control our feelings," said an advertising executive. "Maybe a few of us do cry when we feel very upset about an issue, but most of us don't. Our strong convictions may sometimes come out as emotionality. But that's not a weakness, as far as I'm concerned." A group manager explained, "Men are well defended. They have been taught since childhood to hide their feelings, so they see any sign of emotionality as feminine—and weak."

Most women say that the invisible or "glass" ceiling prevents them from rising to senior and executive positions.

"You can be a star at the mid-management level, but that's it," said a woman director of research. "Men promote other men to the top corporate levels, even if they're mediocre. To have a woman at the top is to lessen the position in many men's eyes. I guess that's why only 3 percent of senior managers in *Fortune* 500 corporations are women."

"You're not ready yet" is usually the answer given to women, regardless of the position they're seeking. "Excuses, excuses, that's all we get, even though we have better experience and credentials than others at that level—or even our bosses," said a public relations manager. "And part of not being ready is that we're not 'clubable'—we can never really be accepted into the male network." A woman marketing analyst concurred: "Women are in staff or service ghettos—the back room. We're the investment analysts, not the portfolio managers; we're in human resources, not in policy making. Men don't let us get ready, because we're not given the jobs that lead to top positions."

Many women say they have left or will leave their jobs because there is no future for them at their companies.

A former computer company executive who left to start her own business said, "A major myth is that women leave jobs only to take care of their kids. That's just not true for many women. Women are leaving because they're not getting ahead or because the corporate atmosphere is so unpleasant."

Many women say that a combination of a corrosive atmosphere and a lack of advancement are major reasons that women leave organizations in greater numbers than men, in addition to the companies' unwillingness to accommodate family needs.

Scenes from the Workplace

The "Glass Ceiling"

Lisa Weber never doubted that she would be a partner in her Wall Street firm. A graduate of a prestigious business school, with a doctorate in economics, she taught briefly at a major university. She was the first woman hired as a market analyst in her well-regarded firm. Within two years she had become one of four senior portfolio managers reporting directly to a senior partner. Her clients give her the highest commendations for her outstanding performance and over the last two years, she has brought in the largest number of new accounts to the firm.

Despite the admiration of her colleagues, and their seeming acceptance of her, there is a disturbing, if flattering, aspect to her job. Most of her peers and some of the partners visit her office during the day to discuss in private her opinions on market performance and financial projections. She enjoys these private sessions but is dismayed that at the weekly staff meetings the CEO, Michael Breyer, usually says something like, "Okay, let's get started and bring Lisa up-to-date on some of the trouble spots." None of her peers or the partners mention that Lisa knows as much as they do about what's going on in the firm. She never protests this slight to her competence and knowledge of firm business, nor does she mention the almost daily private meetings where her advice is sought. As the only woman on the executive level, she prefers to be considered a team player and "one of the boys."

During the past year, one of her peers was promoted to partner, although Lisa's performance clearly surpassed his, as measured by the success of her accounts and the amount of new business she brought to the firm. Having heard no mention of partnership for herself, she approached her boss, one of the partners, and asked about the path to a partnership. He replied, "You're doing great, Lisa, but professors do not partners make. What happens if you are a partner and you make a huge mistake? How would you take it? And what about our clients? There's never been a female partner in the 103 years of our firm."

Shortly thereafter, another woman, Pamela Tobias, was hired as a marketing analyst. Once, when the CEO saw Lisa and Pamela together, he called out to the men, "Hey, guys, two women in one room. That's scary."

During the next six months, Lisa meets several times with the CEO to make her case for a partnership on the basis of her performance. She finally realizes that there is no possibility of change in the foreseeable future and makes a decision to leave and form her own investment firm.

What Went Wrong?

1. Lisa's outstanding contributions to the firm in number of clients won and performance of accounts were not rewarded with a promotion.
2. Lisa's peer, a man whose performance did not equal hers, was promoted to partner while Lisa was not.
3. Despite the fact that Lisa's advice was widely sought, her importance was diminished by the CEO's statement "Let's bring Lisa up-to-date." None of the other men contradicted that statement by mentioning Lisa's valued advice and participation and pointing out that she clearly knew as much as the men, if not more, about the firm's business.
4. When Lisa asked for a promotion, she was rebuffed by her boss's remark that "professors do not partners make," which demeaned her educational experience and style.

5. Lisa was told that it would be too risky for her and the firm if she were made a partner and made a mistake. Her boss accepted the stereotypes that women cannot emotionally take failure and that a man's mistake can be tolerated by clients, whereas a woman's cannot.
6. By making the comment about it's being "scary" to have two senior women in the office, the CEO showed his discomfort with seeing women in senior positions. This undoubtedly reinforced and sanctioned the bias of other members of the firm.

What Should Have Been Done?

1. The firm's top executives should have recognized and publicly acknowledged Lisa's outstanding contributions to the firm, including the number of new accounts she brought in, the performance of her accounts, and the private advice to senior staff that she gave so willingly and that was eagerly sought.
2. One of the partners should have functioned as her mentor so that she would have a real opportunity to become a partner. If Lisa's management style appeared too professorial, the mentor should have first reviewed in his mind, or with other partners, whether her style was indeed detrimental or whether he had only a limited view of what the style should be. Certainly Lisa's style did not affect her ability to bring accounts into the firm. If the mentor did decide that Lisa's mannerisms were a problem, he should have given her specific feedback and coached her on more appropriate and effective behavior for the entrepreneurial world of Wall Street.
3. The firm should have reviewed its policy regarding the hiring and promoting of women to top executive ranks, including taking an honest look at its organizational culture, which may be antagonistic to the full acceptance and recognition of women's contributions and ambitions.

What a Senior Partner or the CEO Might Have Said

"Lisa, your performance with the firm has been outstanding these past two years. I want you to become a partner by the beginning of next year, and I'd like to outline some strategies to do this. During the next few weeks, let's schedule some meeting time so that we can go over some management issues and concerns I have about smoothing the way for your acceptance as the first woman partner at our firm. Second, I'm inviting you to some of the partners' lunch meetings so that we can get to know you in an informal setting. And third, I intend to acknowledge you at our weekly meetings for the tremendous help you've been to all of us."

Pregnancy as a Barrier to Job Status

Marina Soslow is a senior managing director at a manufacturing company. She has worked at the company for ten years, gradually working her way up to a responsible position. She would like to win promotion to a top executive position and has recently finished an M.B.A., which supplements her master's degree in chemical engineering.

Several months ago, she found out she was pregnant. She is reluctant to tell her boss, Roy Bond, the division head, because she knows several other women who were eased out of their positions either before they gave birth or shortly thereafter.

After a meeting with Roy about a new product, Marina mentions her pregnancy and says that she plans to take a three-month leave of absence after her delivery. She begins describing the plans she has carefully worked out for distributing her work. Roy cuts her short and says, "I knew this was going to happen sooner or later—it always does." He said this as if a disaster were about to occur. "There's no point in talking about this now—we'll think about it later."

Marina can tell that he's very annoyed right now about what he thinks is going to happen; she can see his wheels spinning and worries about the implications for her. She thinks, "Doesn't Roy know about the Family and Medical Leave Act of 1993? Legally, this company has to guarantee my job, but I know he can make it very rough for me."

What Went Wrong?

1. Roy didn't discuss with Marina the plans she has made for handling her work during her planned absence.

2. He did not indicate that he was willing to cooperate with Marina on how best to accommodate both Marina and the company, i.e., to ensure her job and maintain the company business.
3. He linked Marina to other women who had left or who he assumed would leave. He conveyed stereotypic thinking about women, implying, "All women get pregnant and leave us in the lurch." He should have made no assumptions about what her pregnancy meant for her work. Although some women leave work and do not return, some return within a few weeks. Others may be away longer. Some women work at home even though they are officially on leave. No two women view managing family and work in the same way. However, many—if not most— women do plan to return to work after giving birth and certainly want to maintain their organization's effectiveness while they are away.

What Should Have Been Done?

1. As a valued employee, Marina should have been congratulated on her pregnancy, and Roy should have indicated some interest in her family life.
2. Roy should have explored with Marina her plans for leaving and her ideas on how they could work cooperatively to ensure that her work would be covered during her absence.
3. He should have assured her of his looking forward to her return and stated that her job would, of course, be in place.
4. Roy should become familiar with the Family and Medical Leave Act of 1993, which, for a company of this size (more than fifty employees), guarantees a worker's right to an unpaid leave of up to twelve weeks.

What the Supervisor Might Have Said

"Congratulations, Marina, on your pregnancy. It's great that you've started planning for your leave. I'd like to help you in any way I can. Let's discuss the work allocation plans you've developed and include some contingency plans if you have to stay out longer.

"I'm delighted that you're planning to come back to work. We really don't want to lose you. Recently, several women in the company have been very successful about accommodating family and work. Our company has been slow in dealing with this important issue, and we're trying to catch up."

Sexual Harassment

Patricia Donfield is a twenty-five-year-old management trainee for a large national food company. She is the only woman among six trainees who are going through an intensive four-week program that will lead to placement as a product manager.

As Patricia enters the room on the first day of training, Hank Stillman, one of the trainees, points to a large picture on the wall that shows a harbor scene, with a sailboat passing a large buoy. He looks Patricia up and down and shouts to the other men, "Hey, now there's three buoys in the room!" The other trainees laugh loudly, and the instructor, the senior director of product development, Dan McKay, says nothing. Patricia's face flushes with embarrassment and in a sarcastic tone she says, "Very funny!"

During the next three weeks, numerous other sexual remarks are made. For example, one of the men says to Dan, "How can we guys concentrate when she's in the room?" Dan laughs and says, "Come on, guys, cool it." Patricia adds, "I'm really tired of this kind of humor. Give me a break." Patricia tries to handle the remarks by ignoring them, protesting, or teasing back. Nothing changes the men's behavior.

But the most alarming incident occurs at an overnight stay at a regional site during the last week of the training program. All of the men trainees appear at her room after dinner, and one of them says, "We're partying here."

Despite her protests, they barge into the room, bottles of liquor in hand. Hank, the most aggressive of the group and its apparent leader, brushes up against her and says, "Come on, Patty, loosen up, we're all going to be working together now.

How're you going to make it here if you're so uptight? This isn't the Girl Scouts." Patricia tells the group to leave, first lightly and then firmly, but to no avail. The men continue to laugh and pass drinks around. Hank starts dancing seductively toward her. Patricia becomes frightened, leaves the hotel room, and calls Dan, the senior manager and program instructor, who meets her in the lobby.

"This is too much," Patricia says to Dan. "I want these guys removed from my room, and the sexual innuendo and remarks have got to stop." Dan says, "Patty, calm down. They're guys just having a good time. The program's pretty intensive, and they're just loosening up. The food industry's a macho place, and you're going to be dealing with these kinds of guys all the time. I think you can make it here if you laugh it off and don't overreact. They're just trying to get your dander up, but it doesn't mean a thing. I'll take care of this situation now, but I won't always be here to fix things up. That's up to you from now on."

As Dan goes to the room to tell the men to stop partying, Patricia says to herself, "I can see I'm not going to get to the top here. I may even be out of the training program altogether if I make a formal sexual harassment complaint. I know that's career suicide. What a choice!"

What Went Wrong?

1. Patricia is being subjected by her coworkers to a hostile and intimidating work environment, which legally constitutes sexual harassment.
2. Dan, the manager, ignored the sexual remarks made to Patricia in his presence.
3. He dismissed Patricia's complaint as unimportant and an overreaction.
4. The manager stated that it was Patricia's responsibility to cope with the "macho" atmosphere of the organization.
5. Although Dan said he would take care of the situation in the hotel room, he said that he would assume no further responsibility for preventing future incidents.

What Should Have Been Done?

1. When the manager first heard the sexual comments, he should have intervened, saying they were inappropriate and could constitute sexual harassment. At a minimum, his first action should have been a strong expression of disapproval and an insistence that the men stop their offensive comments.
2. The manager should have assured Patricia that he took her complaint seriously and that he would act on it. He should have gotten all the facts from her about her coworkers' alleged offensive behavior.
3. He should have informed Patricia of her right to file a formal complaint immediately and certainly if the men's behavior did not cease.
4. He should have spoken to the men trainees about the allegations and the seriousness of the complaint. He should have listened to their explanation of their behavior but explained that, whatever their intent, their behavior constituted sexual harassment and could have legal consequences.
5. Dan, as manager, must know that he and the organization have a legal responsibility to prevent unwanted sexual behavior and to ensure for all employees—men and women alike—a work environment free from sexual harassment. Dan should advise the top management of the need for a firm policy on sexual harassment: a widely distributed, written policy statement; training for employees; and procedures for handling grievances from employees.

What the Manager Might Have Said to Patricia

The following illustration assumes that the supervisor was not a direct observer of any sexual harassment. If he had been, he should, of course, have taken immediate action.

"Patricia, I'm glad you came to me about this matter. Please tell me exactly what happened in this incident, as well as anything that happened before." If Patricia doesn't include it in her description, Dan should ask, "Did Hank and the others know their behavior was objectionable to you? If you told them, what was their reaction?"

After Patricia describes what happened, Dan should continue, "I don't know what Hank and the others' intentions were. I know they're a pretty macho bunch in this business, which has been all male, but the behavior you've described is sexual harassment, that is, creating a hostile and intimidating work atmosphere. I intend to meet with the men in the group immediately, tell them of the seriousness of the charges, and get the facts as they perceive them. I will, of course, tell them that the behavior you described must stop.

"You'll have to decide whether you want to follow company procedures and file a formal complaint now or wait to see if the behavior stops. In any case, I want to meet with you next week to follow up."

What the Manager Might Have Said to the Men Trainees

"I've asked you all to see me to discuss an allegation of sexual harassment." Dan should describe the facts as described by Patricia and ask for the men's description of the facts.

After hearing their side, Dan should continue, "You might not realize the seriousness of this behavior, because you thought you were just fooling around. But let's be clear about this. It's not the intent that's the issue. It's the effect or the impact of your behavior that's the issue, and in this case, it was perceived as intimidating, hostile, and unwanted. And it clearly seems that way to me. This constitutes sexual harassment. I expect this behavior to cease immediately. From now on your interactions with Patricia will be on a professional, harassment-free basis. To do otherwise is not only to jeopardize your placement in our managerial slots but to make yourselves—as well as me—subject to legal action. We'll be lucky if she doesn't take any action just on the basis of what's already happened."

Lack of Inclusion and Credibility

Lori Bradley, an experienced probation officer, is meeting with Ted Stolze and Ian Bateson, two other probation officers, and their supervisor, Len Duggan, the assistant chief of probation. They are planning an orientation session for new probation officers on how to prepare investigative reports for the court.

As Lori enters the room, the two other probation officers are throwing paper clips at each other and laughing about a major play in the previous night's NFL championship game. They continue talking as she enters the room, ignoring her. When Len, the assistant chief, enters, the two men include him in their talk about the game.

After a few minutes, Len says, "Okay, let's get down to business and start planning the orientation session. Any ideas?"

Lori says, "I looked again at the session prepared by Columbia County, which was described at our last meeting, and I think we should use that. It worked well for them and seems to fit our county." No one looks at Lori or responds to her, but Ted begins making some suggestions for a different idea and the others follow up with questions to him. After problems arise with Ted's suggestion, Ian then says, "My idea would be to go for the Columbia County plan; that would work best here." Len, the assistant chief, says, "Ian, I'll go with your judgment." Ted says, "Me, too. Great idea, Ian."

Lori breaks in, "But that's what I proposed initially, and you just ignored me." Ian says, "Stop being so sensitive, Lori. We're supposed to be a team here."

What Went Wrong?

1. The two men coworkers excluded Lori from their horseplay and their talk about the sports game. Len, the supervisor, also took no action to include Lori in the premeeting banter.
2. All of the men ignored Lori's suggestion for the orientation program.
3. Ian took credit for the recommendation that Lori had made earlier. Len, the supervisor, and Ted went along with giving Ian credit for the idea instead of Lori.
4. When Lori spoke up for herself, she was accused of being sensitive and not being a team player. Len, the supervisor, didn't support Lori.

5. The men's behavior could inhibit Lori from making suggestions in future sessions; she might assume that her viewpoint will be ignored or that someone else will be given credit for her suggestions.

What Should Have Been Done?

1. The men coworkers should have acknowledged Lori's presence and included her in the conversation before the meeting started.
2. Len, the assistant chief, should have served as a model for behavior in the group. Even if Ian deflected the conversation from Lori, Len should have specifically acknowledged Lori's suggestion, both when she made it initially and when the group decided to adopt it. He should be aware that lack of acknowledgment of a woman's contribution— or anyone's—can damage self-confidence and overall confidence in the group's functioning. Ultimately, this lack of confidence will be reflected in poor morale and limited mobility within the organization.

What Might Have Been Said

After Ian made the same suggestion that Lori did, Len might have said, "I'm glad you agree with the idea that Lori presented before. I'll go along, too. It's great that we see things together on this planning team."

Summary

The major barriers for women depicted in the workplace examples are: (1) the "glass ceiling" faced by women near the top of the organizational hierarchy, (2) the negative implications for a woman's career when she discloses her pregnancy, (3) the use of subtle or blatant sexual harassment to intimidate women, particularly in formerly all-male work settings, and (4) the reluctance of men to listen to women and to acknowledge their competence and achievement.

Chapter 11
White Men

White men represent 39.2 percent of the population and 47 percent of the workforce. But these numbers in no way reflect the power and dominance white men have traditionally had in the workplace and in society in general. They constitute 77 percent of the members of Congress, 92 percent of state governors, 70 percent of tenured college faculty, almost 90 percent of daily newspaper editors, and 77 percent of television news directors.[1]

Despite these statistics, the dynamics of the workplace are changing rapidly. Indeed, these changes are a primary reason for this book. As indicated in Chapter 1, it is predicted that by 2000, only 15 percent of the new entrants to the workforce will be American-born, English-speaking white men.

White men are seeing incursions by others into areas that were once exclusively their domain. Racial minorities and women are seen more and more often across the entire spectrum of the workplace, whether on police forces or in executive suites.

There is a reality that in many areas of the workforce it has become harder for a white man to compete for a job, particularly below the senior executive level. At one time, white men competed only with one another. Now women and racial minorities are also in the competitive pool.

It is not only that the competition is greater. The 1990s are a transitional time for gender roles in our society. Women truck-drivers and executives seem like an anomaly to many men in these changing times, with sex roles blurred and unclear. Many men were socialized into assuming that only men would hold jobs requiring physical strength and dexterity and that only men were supposed to hold the superior positions in organizations.

Physical strength and dominance in the organizational hierarchy were part of male identity.

Many white men feel that the category *white male* is too limited to be useful because it ignores ethnicity, social class, and age, all of which affect experiences and opportunities. Nonetheless, our assumption in this chapter is that this group—white, European, physically able, heterosexual men—has defined the workplace norms and standards by which all other group members are judged. Some of those standards have been affected by the socialization of white men to be physically strong, competitive, aggressive, direct, dominant, knowledgeable, and emotionally restrained.

Being white and male has always conferred automatic advantage. The sense of loss and disorientation experienced by white men today because of the changes in their position in the workplace is creating new dilemmas. Further, since many of the issues discussed in this chapter have to do with gender roles, they tend to apply to all men, regardless of color or ethnicity.

Voices of White Males in the Workplace

Many white men resent having others assume they are all racists or sexists and being seen uniformly as the "enemy."

A food service manager said, "If we talked about others the way we're talked about, we'd be considered bigots." Another white manager added, "We're now the new victims; one lousy system of stereotyping has been traded for another. White heterosexual male-bashing has become fashionable."

A human resources manager said, "Yes, some white males are blatant racists and sexists, but there is a very broad spectrum of views out there. A lot of men may be insensitive to blacks and other minorities or guilty of putting women down, but that doesn't mean we're all bad. I can accept criticism of a specific behavior but not broad categorizations. Like women, blacks, and others, we're individuals and want to be judged that way."

"This indiscriminate white male-bashing has got to stop," said a white housing administrator. He described how he had spent his entire professional career in a multiracial workplace developing low-cost housing, and a new black employee at a staff meeting denounced him as "just another white racist" when they disagreed. He added, "Even though I know it's not a personal thing, I was in a rage. I don't know if we'll ever get it together."

Many white men say that because others assume they're racists and sexists, they're afraid to say anything for fear of being misinterpreted.

"I'm always worried about how I was heard. How will I be interpreted? Did I say the wrong thing?" said a white loan officer. Another white bank manager described a board meeting in a black community. "I was making some suggestions about loan applications, and someone interrupted and said, 'We're not going to buy into what you whites want.' " "It gets so you're afraid to open your mouth," agreed a supervisor in a printing company. "It's 'you're white, so you're wrong.' Because of this, I've chosen silence."

A sales manager said, "We're told by many women, 'You're not one of us. You don't get it.' But if that's true, how can we ever communicate honestly or supervise each other effectively?"

Some white men feel that when they "don't get it," women and minorities are reluctant to explain their positions. "They assume we're all hopeless and write us off as impossible instead of helping us to 'get it.' "

Some white men say they are concerned that African-Americans and Latinos automatically consider white male supervision to be patronizing.

"I can feel the resentment," said a white supervisor in a social service agency, "and I'm always on the defensive when I'm giving feedback. The dilemma is that society has made the power relationships unequal between whites and people of color, and that's hard to undo in a supervisory encounter. I have a specific expertise that I want to share with my staff, and I'm made to feel like a colonial imperialist."

A white salesman is reluctant to make suggestions to his black peers because once, when he did, a black man bristled as if he had been insulted. "I would like to discuss the merits of my suggestions," said a computer analyst. "But I've become self-conscious about saying anything because I may be seen like a know-it-all or, worse, a racist. I honestly don't know how to deal with that defensiveness about power."

Many white men, especially blue-collar workers in traditional occupations, infer that their manhood is being taken away when women enter the workplace and perform the same job.

Many men expressed the feeling that physical strength is an essential part of manhood and say that if women can demonstrate the same strength, they feel castrated and "demanned." A foreman of a construction company said, "Our manhood is defined by our strength. If women can do the same thing, then what does it mean to be a man?"

"There is a bond and a sense of communion between men who do hard, physical labor. That bond is now broken," said a trucking company supervisor.

Many white men say that others assume they have power in the organization, but in actuality they often feel powerless and vulnerable.

A white engineer in a large electronics company said plaintively, "I hear all this talk from women and blacks about how white men have all the power in our society, and I wonder who they're talking about. I know it's not me. I'm holding onto my job by my fingernails. There's a tremendous amount of competition—from other white men, and also from women and minorities. I always feel I'm at the mercy of the top guys who run the organizations. Maybe the CEOs and the top execs, who are mostly white men, have the power, but not white guys on my level."

Several men felt that class and religious issues, as well as ethnicity, are often overlooked when discussing white men. "I went to a small Catholic college in upstate New York, and I feel as if I can never compete in my corporate bank setting, despite my M.B.A. from a local city college. I'm third-generation Irish-German, from a working-class background, and I probably feel as estranged from the 'establishment' Ivy Leaguers as most of the women and blacks do. In fact, some of the black male Columbia law graduates or M.B.A.s seem to have more in common with the top guys than I do, yet there is that idea that all white guys have it made."

A white probation officer claims he was asked recently by a black coworker, "So how come you're in this rotten job? You white guys have all the marbles—what's your excuse for being here?" The white officer claims he said to his coworker, "I killed myself to get through college and pass the exam for this job. Just because I'm white doesn't mean I can do whatever I want." He, like many others, had no sense of feeling "empowered" and resented being ridiculed for not "doing better" or for "having all the cards or marbles."

Many white men say they are unsure of the proper etiquette in working with women; yet they are attacked for being paternalistic or sexist if they do or say the wrong thing.

When a white male computer programmer offered to lift some heavy video equipment for a female trainer, she said sarcastically, "Well, thank you, Sir Galahad, but I don't think I'm that weak." Afterward, he said he wondered, "Would I have offered to help another man? Probably not. But was I flaunting my superior strength instead of just being helpful? I began to wonder."

A section chief in a government agency described an incident when he opened the door for a female colleague and she said, "Are you trying to make a political statement?" The man said he was really struggling with how to act because he grew up in a traditional home and was taught to be polite and courteous to women.

Many white men say that others don't understand their inability to show lack of knowledge.

A white male financial planner said, "In addition to not knowing what to do, it's hard for me to explain that I don't understand the new rules and to ask for advice. I can't say I'm uncertain or unsure. That's not being 'manly.' I remember my father teaching me that and acting that way himself."

Many white men in senior positions say that they are dissuaded from mentoring women because it is sometimes perceived as sexual harassment or sexual involvement.

A senior executive in the pharmaceutical industry described how he had worked very closely with a woman team leader in his division, grooming her to become a director. "It's true I spent a lot of time coaching her on financial management and bringing her along to senior staff meetings, but I thought I was doing exactly what you are supposed to do in the mentoring process. But when she was promoted to director, I heard lots of gossip that she got the promotion because there was something going on between us. She denied it, and so did I. But despite the denials, it was really hard to shake that rumor. It was a no-win rumor. Some of my male colleagues assumed I was being used by her to get ahead; some of the women thought Jane had been used by me to get ahead. I guess to mentor successfully, you pretty much have to be a eunuch."

Several male sales executives said they try to never be alone with a woman, especially a subordinate, even for lunch, because of these kinds of rumors. Other senior managers say they are recommending that only senior women managers mentor the younger women.

Many white men say they are conflicted about the problems in accommodating women on family and work issues.

A director of clinical services in a large medical center said that he had trouble when women residents had to take off extra time for child-care or family emergencies. "I'm finding that it's a pain to constantly rearrange the schedules to accommodate the women here. And on top of that, my efforts are often not appreciated by them. It's assumed the rules are my doing, which is not the case. I also have a nagging feeling that some of the women aren't doing all they can to assume their responsibilities in making adequate family arrangements."

Other white male managers in corporate settings described similar problems in covering the work of women during family emergencies. One manager in a manufacturing company said, "The company should make changes. I understand the needs of the women, but I'm getting squeezed from two sides—my boss demanding that I meet deadlines and the women pressing me to let them leave work early or take off."

Some white men say they feel they have to fight a battle of mixed loyalties in the changing workplace.

A municipal firefighter said, "Women and some blacks don't understand that it's considered breaking ranks if we're friendly with them. You can't imagine the razzing I got when I supported a woman firefighter complaining about unfair treatment. I was called traitor by more than one guy."

A white police officer described the flip side of this. He said, "I've tried to break into the black crowd in my department, and I feel frozen out. I know a couple of the guys who are really friendly one-on-one, but they don't want to be seen with me too much in front of their buddies. Some of the blacks feel they're being disloyal to the 'brotherhood' if they hang around with whites too much."

Many white men say that their jobs are made much harder because they have to learn a new management style to accommodate the new groups in the workplace.

A consumer products manager said that it was not just the hiring but the whole managing process that was difficult. He said, "White managers, especially middle-aged ones, expect workers to come from the same background, have the same expectations and values. I can feel much more confident and comfortable managing a white man than managing women or minorities. When dealing with them, I feel as if I'm working with an unknown quantity. This makes me more tentative, less secure. I feel I have to learn new skills and knowledge, in addition to having the normal sensitivity a good manager should have. Before, people looked like you, talked like you, and aspired like you—it was easier."

Many white men say they do not understand the definition of sexual harassment.

Although most men claim they understand blatant sexual harassment like "groping, grabbing, and forcing" or quid-pro-quo demands from supervisors, many men say they do not understand the more subtle aspects of sexual harassment.

A university professor claimed that at the end of a conference with a student, he gently put his arm around her shoulder because she seemed upset. She bolted from him and shouted, "Get your hands off me!" My door was open, there was another student right outside, and I was terribly embarrassed. I realized that any form of touching can be misconstrued and I never did that again."

Several men said they don't know the rules on off-color jokes. A marketing representative said, "Lots of the women here tell plenty of them and laugh at ours; others take great offense and tell us they're going to report us. I feel like there's a double standard. The women can tell dirty jokes to us, but we can't do the same with them."

Some men claim they are not sure how to respond when women flirt with them. An account executive in a brokerage house said, "I feel like I could be entrapped. I'm just not taking any chances."

Many white men say they are uncomfortable giving feedback to women.

A fifty-year-old white male architect said, "It may be sexist, but I was brought up to be protective of women, and I feel that I want to cover their mistakes rather than confront them directly. I know this is seen as patronizing and assumes women can't take it, but it's hard to change the patterns I grew up with."

A project leader in an insurance company said, "If I'm as direct with a woman as I am with a man, she may accuse me of sex discrimination and say I'm too critical of her because she's a woman. Yet other guys have been told they're condescending if they're lenient in their feedback. I feel I can't win and as if I need to be trained in a new language when I talk to women at work."

Many white men say that the laws that help women and other protected groups may be justified but are difficult to accept.

"I know there's been discrimination in the past and things have to change, but the remedy seems to be all at the expense of the white man. I've seen too many terrific white guys passed over for a job or promotion just to make room for a woman, a black, or a Latino who doesn't have as much experience. Why do we have to pay for the atrocities of slavery and every other social injustice?"

A newspaper writer said, "Yes, we're mad, scared, and pained by the changes of the past thirty years—the women's movement and the civil rights laws make us feel as if we're being eclipsed by everyone. There's a real sense of loss in status. In my head, I know some of these changes are needed, but don't expect me to go gently into the night."

A mid-level state manager said, "We're on the other end of the stick now—we see ourselves knocking ourselves out and not getting recognition or a promotion we deserve. Why should I bother killing myself at work? Many of us are just lowering our sights and accepting the situation. To protest is like shoveling sand against the tide. The real loser is the agency I work for, since I'm just not trying as hard as I used to."

An assistant director of a nonprofit agency described a young black woman's success in obtaining a top position in a government agency. He said sadly, "She sees that any option is open to her. I'm glad for her, but in this shrinking economy, my aspirations are very limited. I feel my crime is that I'm a white middle-aged man."

Scenes from the Workplace

Complaint of Reverse Discrimination

Richard Green, a white male supervisor in an aerospace company, applies for a middle management position that has recently been posted. A month later he hears that Derrick Moore, a black coworker, has been selected for this position, which has never been held by a member of a minority before. Although Richard respects Derrick, who has strong academic credentials, he knows his experience outweighs Derrick's.

After Derrick's appointment, Richard speaks to the department head, Nina Stevens, to discuss his future in the company. He says, "I don't understand why Derrick got the job instead of me. I've been here two years longer, and my computer background and supervisory experience are stronger than his. Do you have to be a black to be promoted around here?"

Nina says, "I think Derrick will be a fine manager. And

besides, there are new realities in the workplace, and you'll have to get used to it."

What Went Wrong?

1. Nina, the department head, did not acknowledge Richard's accomplishments and his contributions to the firm.
2. She did not discuss his disappointment over not being promoted and his resentment of a policy that seemed to favor women and minorities.
3. Nina gave Richard no encouragement about his future career goals.
4. She did not explain the company policy on affirmative action.

What Should Have Been Done?

1. Nina should have told Richard that he is a valued employee and that his contributions to the department are recognized and appreciated.
2. Richard should have been assured that he is promotable and that when another opportunity comes up, he will certainly be considered. However, he must recognize that the shrinking economy and affirmative action considerations may delay that opportunity.
3. Nina should have explained the definition of and the reasons for affirmative action, which emphasizes reaching out to minorities and women who are qualified to do the job. She should have pointed out that although affirmative action is a government policy designed to overcome past injustices in employment opportunities, it is also a beneficial employment practice for the organization. In addition, she should have explained that hiring women and minorities has a sound business rationale, since it reflects the customer base in a multicultural society and provides a broadened perspective that is needed in organizational policy and decision making.

What the Manager Might Have Said

"Richard, I can understand your disappointment about not being selected as a manager in the department. As you probably know from our meetings together, the company recognizes your strong contributions, and we highly value you as an employee. I don't know when another promotional opportunity will come up, but when it does, I hope you will apply again.

"What makes the situation so frustrating for all of us is that the economy has affected our company badly, as you know, and managerial slots are limited. In addition, there is an affirmative action mandate at this company for hiring and promoting qualified women and minority workers and workers with disabilities.

"I want to talk to you about your perception that Derrick was promoted only because he's black. Yes, that was a consideration, but, first and foremost, Derrick's skills and past performance at the company qualify him for this job. He also can relate to our expanding customer base and brings a perspective that's been missing in our organization and needs to be heard.

"Affirmative action has long been misunderstood. It means expanding our outreach to actively recruit and promote women and minorities who are qualified, and Derrick certainly meets that criterion.

"I know the decision may still seem unfair to you, but I hope that you can understand its importance to our company goals on several levels and that you will continue to give our department your full commitment, as you have in the past."

Sexism or Personality Style?

Eric Giles, a white man, is the creative director in a large advertising firm. Stephanie Rostow has worked as an artist in his department for the past six months. On several occasions, he criticizes her work and asks her to come up with different concepts. His criticism is given in a direct, no-nonsense manner that she interprets as demeaning. Stephanie has just asked Eric to give her an assignment for a new client. He tells her, "I'm giving it to Phil since we're under such time pressure." The same day, he tells Stephanie that he's cutting out her portion of a presentation to another client. She thinks, "He wouldn't have done that to me if I were a man."

Several days later, Eric is called into the office of Ruth Smiley, the senior vice president. "Listen, Eric, Stephanie is complaining to me about you. I want to nip this in the bud before we have some kind of sex discrimination claim here." When Eric asks what he is being charged with, Ruth tells him, "Eric, it's your whole attitude; you don't give her a chance. You're really picking on her for every little thing; she feels that you wouldn't treat a man that way." When Eric protests and reminds Ruth about his past positive experiences in working with and promoting women, Ruth shrugs and says, "I suggest you talk to her directly. You should be able to handle this on your own."

Eric is uncomfortable bringing the matter to Stephanie, but he forces himself to stop by her desk and say, "What did you say to Ruth? I'd like to know if I'm doing something that bothers you." Stephanie seems embarrassed and says, "If you don't get it, I can't really explain it to you. Just give me a break." Eric is confused and angry.

What Went Wrong?

1. Ruth, the senior vice president, didn't describe Stephanie's complaints and did not ask Eric for his view of the events described.
2. She didn't help Eric deal with Stephanie as a supervisee in his department.
3. She didn't help Stephanie deal with Eric as a supervisor.

What Should Have Been Done?

1. Ruth should have had a detailed description from Stephanie of Eric's behavior and should have described these charges to Eric. She should then have heard Eric's side of the story.
2. Ruth should have viewed the complaint in the context of Eric's long history in the department and acknowledged his reputation for fairness and effectiveness with all employees, men and women, despite his direct and some-

times brusque style. She should have explained to Eric that Stephanie might have viewed his style as being discriminatory toward her because she was a woman, particularly since she was the only woman in the unit.

3. Ruth should have discussed with Stephanie the difference between interpersonal style and sex discrimination, which is defined as detrimental employment actions based solely on gender. She could have explained to Stephanie that Eric's behavior was probably a reflection of his personality, since in the past he had promoted women in his department. She should have encouraged Stephanie to speak directly to Eric and tell him when she felt that he was being unfair to her.

What Ruth Might Have Said to Stephanie

"Stephanie, after hearing both your side and Eric's side of the story, I'd like to make some suggestions. You may not know of Eric's reputation in the company. He is known for having a very direct style, but he is always seen as fair, by both men and women. Unlike a few of the men in the company, Eric has never had complaints brought against him by women. I suggest that you speak to Eric directly and specifically about what you see as unfair. I hope you can work this out with Eric directly, but my door is always open to you."

What Ruth Might Have Said to Eric

"Eric, I'd like to help resolve Stephanie's concerns. As you know, sex discrimination is not condoned in this organization, and I know your record has been fine in working with and promoting women in the past. So instead of sex discrimination, as she suspects, I'd like to assume that it's more a matter of a typical supervisor-supervisee communication problem. I would encourage you to meet informally with Stephanie, perhaps over coffee or lunch, and explain the reasons for the decisions you've taken about her work. I'm encouraging her—as I think you should, too—to come to you directly whenever she doesn't understand or agree with your decisions."

"Whose Side Are You On?"

Stuart Snyder, a white man, is the assistant general manager of a large hotel. He supervises two women, Beth Quinn, who is head of the banquets department, and Sylvia Obermeyer, a manager in the accounts division. Both women have young children. Although they are willing to work late when needed, they each have asked Stuart to give them enough advance notice so that they can make arrangements for child care. Beth is a single parent, and Sylvia's husband works evenings on the local newspaper. Both Beth and Sylvia are totally dependent on their child-care providers for the supervision of their children.

Stuart is very sympathetic to the concerns of Beth and Sylvia. He understands their dilemma, particularly since he, too, has young children and his wife works. She is a teacher, however, and always gets home before Stuart. Although Stuart has spoken to the general manager, Henry Ross, about trying to eliminate emergency meetings after 5 P.M., Henry still calls last-minute meetings after 5 P.M. several times a month for key staff, which includes Beth and Sylvia. Both women have told Stuart, to whom they report directly, that they get knots in their stomachs whenever they hear about these unexpected meetings because they don't know if they can get coverage for their children at the last minute.

After the most recent "emergency" meeting, Stuart speaks to Henry and says he doesn't understand why the meetings can't be held earlier in the day. "I think we have to understand the concerns of the women on our staff." Henry is furious and says to Stuart, "Well, I guess I know who wears the pants in your family. We're running a business here, not a nursery. Either the women are professionals or they're not. If you can't control your staff, maybe I'd better look for someone who can. Whose side are you on, anyway? In these times, we guys have to stick together."

Stuart doesn't want to jeopardize his job, so he doesn't say anything further to Henry.

When Stuart tells the women that he is unable to change Henry's policy on emergency meetings, they look at him rather contemptuously. "Listen, you're the assistant manager. I can't believe that you don't have input. Are you really on our side or are you just going through the motions?"

Stuart is in a dilemma because he doesn't want to "bad-mouth" Henry, his boss, to the women. Although he knows the women are right, he also resents them because they think he has more power than he does to change policy.

What Went Wrong?

1. The general manager, Henry Ross, seemed to define Stuart's masculinity in terms of his being in control of women ("I guess I know who wears the pants in your family.").
2. Henry also tried to polarize relationships between men and women by asking Stuart whose side he was on. He implied that the dispute wasn't just management versus these two women but also a male-female issue.
3. Henry should have realized that not all men feel the same way as he does about women and their roles in the workplace. Stuart feels more sympathetic to the women than does Henry.
4. Beth and Sylvia were not sympathetic to Stuart's dilemma. They stereotyped Stuart in two ways: (1) they assumed he was not really interested in their welfare, and (2) they assumed that he had more power in the organization than he in fact did.

What Should Have Been Done?

1. Henry should have realized that the reality of the workplace has changed. Both men and women have family as well as job responsibilities. The challenge is not to sacrifice one for the other, but to see how the two can be accommodated.
2. Henry should analyze whether it is necessary to call meetings on the spur of the moment after 5 P.M. If it is, does everyone have to attend, or can it be a select group of managers? If it is not essential to have all the meetings after 5 P.M., they should be rescheduled during the working day.

3. Henry should not have dealt with the problem by polarizing relationships between the men and the women on the staff. They are all working for the hotel to ensure that it is as successful as possible. Problems should be discussed in terms of the substance of the issue, not in terms of extraneous issues such as dominance and control or polarization of the sexes.
4. Beth and Sylvia should have worked collaboratively with Stuart to come up with some alternative solutions for dealing with last-minute emergency meetings.

What the General Manager Might Have Said

"I've called the senior staff together because I need your help in dealing with last-minute issues. There are times when I need to meet with key people on a moment's notice, but I know this creates problems for staff with family responsibilities. Stuart, as assistant manager, I'd like you to set up a meeting with the senior staff and come up with recommendations on how we can handle staff communication and the redistribution of job functions to meet the needs of the hotel and our staff."

Summary

The workplace examples in this chapter illustrate the sense of loss and frustration felt by white men who feel that laws and policies favor other groups at their expense. Adjusting to a workforce that no longer comprises only white men requires new management skills and styles to prevent behavior that can be construed as sexist or racist.

Part Three
Guidelines for Better Relationships

Chapter 12

When You Are Not a Member of the Dominant Group in Your Organization—When You Are "The Other"

When we listen to the voices from the diverse workforce, we hear a variety of experiences—offenses, injustices, and misunderstandings. Despite the barriers to full access and workplace equity, however, many members of minority groups in the workplace learn to survive and even to triumph.

How do they cope? Interviews with members of all groups reveal surprisingly similar strategies for dealing with an unresponsive, alien, or hostile environment. These are some of the key strategies.

- *Never assume that the workplace is completely hostile.* There may be people out there of whom you are unaware who can help you and who want you to succeed.
- *Find a mentor or friend in the organization who is in the dominant group.* Use that person as a resource. Ask for information about the informal norms, history, and practices of the organization.
- *Recognize that because of your group identity, you have something distinctive and important to offer.* Be a resource in your organization to a mentor, a friend, or your boss, and share

aspects of your group tendencies that can be helpful in the workplace.

- *Join a network or caucus of your own group.* Share "war stories" and strategies. Use the emotional support from your group, and act from that strength.
- *Don't allow yourself always to be the representative of your group.* Don't be drawn into always speaking on behalf of your group, especially if you don't speak on other issues.
- *Stress what you have in common with coworkers and managers.* Emphasize your desire to be productive and improve the organization's effectiveness. Think in terms of "we," not "me and them."
- *Try to find the humor in common work experiences.* Laughter is therapeutic when shared. Explain your group's style of humor if it is different from that of other groups.
- *Realize that not every slight or misunderstanding is necessarily racist, sexist, or discriminatory.* Slights and misunderstandings may be a result of another person's personality, a norm of the organization, or a reaction to something you have done. See if there is a pattern to the behavior, and check your perceptions with others whom you trust.
- *Recognize clearly sexist, racist, and other discriminatory or stereotypic remarks or behavior.* Control your rage, and state that you don't appreciate the remark or that you don't agree with it. Stand up for other groups that are stereotyped, as well as your own. Do this in a way that does not personally attack the other person.
- *Know the legal and organizational rights that protect you in the workplace.* Be prepared to seek remedies as needed.
- *Welcome and ask for feedback.* Ask, "How do I need to improve?" and "How can I advance further in the organization?"
- *Try to perfect your English.* Remember that proficiency in written and verbal skills is a career booster. Tell others about your efforts.
- *Speak up and ask questions about what you don't know.* Don't sit back and do nothing because of insecurity or attempt to do a job without clear guidelines.
- *Let others know of your accomplishments.* Document them in

writing, if necessary. This is important, even though it may be uncomfortable for you, so bear the discomfort.

- *Ask for what you want.* If you need more resources, additional training, more or less feedback, or an opportunity for advancement, tell your boss. Don't expect that your boss will automatically know what you want and that she or he will take care of it. Take responsibility for making your needs known.
- *Be aware of your own stereotypes of others.* Recognize the diversity within your organization. Don't exclude others from your network. Acknowledge the support of others.
- *Gain visibility in organizational life.* Be active in organizational committees and functions.
- *When you move up in the organization, keep a connection to others in your group.* Don't forget your sources of support. Be a mentor to others coming up.
- *Try to understand and learn from the perspectives of others in the organization, just as you want others to understand and learn from you.*
- *Have a vision for yourself.* Look at role models from your group and from others. Others in your group have made it in the workplace.

Chapter 13

When You Are the Manager or Supervisor

The preceding chapters in this book describe common workplace experiences of several different groups of workers and suggest ways that managers might respond to specific issues pertinent to each group. Imbedded in the specific "how-to's" for each group are general guidelines for understanding, valuing, and utilizing diversity. These guidelines apply to all groups.

- *Approach every employee as an individual.* Although members of different groups may be diverse in appearance, speech, values, beliefs, and behaviors, they have many things in common that cut across different groups. In fact, there can be as many differences within a group as there are between groups. Therefore, you cannot automatically make assumptions about someone on the basis of group identity.
- *Understand that cultural tendencies such as language, mannerisms, and communication patterns are not necessarily indicators of a worker's performance and capabilities.* Within each group there is a range of people, from those who are highly qualified to those who are not qualified for a given position. Managers must understand cultural differences and not allow them to cloud judgments of competence and motivation.
- *Recognize and confront the issue of discomfort—your own and others'—in dealing with a diverse workforce.* Be a role model of acceptance by including all workers in social situations, using inclusive language, structuring work teams for projects, coaching all staff on the work norms of the organiza-

tion, stressing a team atmosphere, and making clear that everyone is in the running for opportunities in the organization.

- *Appreciate and utilize the different perspectives and styles of diverse workers.* All workers want to succeed on the job and to be accepted by the organization, but they also want to maintain their own senses of identity and have their special perspectives and assets acknowledged and appreciated. It's important not simply to tolerate different perspectives but to see them as definite *assets*.
- *Convey clearly your expectations for the work unit, while at the same time recognizing group differences in communication and perspective.* Workers may have different perspectives on a number of issues, including participation in meetings, leadership style, tolerance for bureaucracy and hierarchy, style of dressing, use of English only, and punctuality. The task for the manager is to determine on which of these issues differences can be accommodated or utilized and on which they may interfere with work requirements. In any case, it is the manager's responsibility to clarify and explain the expectations of the organization and to make sure that workers understand the expectations.
- *Use equal performance standards for all workers.* Too often managers' standards for workers in the groups described in this book are either too high or too low. Managers expect some workers to be superstars and expect too little from others. Check your judgments to make sure that you are not magnifying deficits or overlooking problems that legitimately require feedback and correction. Remember that the person who seems different may stand out because there are so few of his or her group in the workplace, allowing any errors to be easily noticed, highlighted, and magnified. On the other hand, don't overlook poor performance because you expect too little or are uncomfortable about giving needed feedback. Instead, help the worker to meet your standard.
- *Provide feedback often and equally to all members of the workforce.* Your failure to give legitimate feedback because you fear being labeled sexist, racist, or discriminatory in some other

way demeans the importance of the worker's career goals and expectations.

- *Openly support the competencies and contribution of workers from all groups.* Many times it is only members of the dominant culture who receive recognition. It is essential that the credentials of new employees be openly stated and that the achievements of all workers be acknowledged when appropriate.
- *Know the federal, state, and municipal legislation that ensures equal opportunity in employment.* Some key federal laws are:
  —Equal Pay Act of 1963, which prohibits discrimination in wages on the basis of gender.
  —Civil Rights Act of 1964, Title VII, which prohibits discrimination in employment based on race, sex, color, religion, or national origin. Sexual harassment is considered a form of sex discrimination under this act as a result of a 1986 Supreme Court decision.
  —Age Discrimination in Employment Act of 1967, which prohibits discrimination for workers age 40 and over.
  —Pregnancy Discrimination Act of 1978, which makes it illegal to discriminate on the basis of pregnancy.
  —Americans with Disabilities Act (ADA) of 1990, which prohibits discrimination in employment against people with physical or mental disabilities if they are able to perform the job with "reasonable accommodations."
  —Civil Rights Act of 1991, which restores the intent of the Civil Rights Act of 1964 regarding employment discrimination. The 1964 act had been weakened by several U.S. Supreme Court decisions. The 1991 act also adds the right to seek damages and to request a jury trial for workers in several protected groups.
  —The Family and Medical Leave Act of 1993, which grants employees in companies with fifty or more workers the right to take up to twelve weeks of unpaid leave for the birth of a child or the illness of a family member.
- *Be aware of subtle and systemic institutional discrimination, intentional or unintentional, that pigeonholes and limits opportunities for members of groups other than those in the dominant culture.* Ask yourself these questions:

—Are there equal opportunities for training and acquiring new skills?

—Are certain positions seen as suitable only for members of certain groups?

- *Confront racist, sexist, or other stereotypic or discriminatory behavior.* Make your position clear by openly stating that neither you nor the company will tolerate discrimination in the workplace.

- *Become comfortable asking questions about preferred terminology or interactions.* Since you can't be an expert on all groups, make it known that you welcome information and feedback, particularly if you have inadvertently made an insensitive or inappropriate remark that may have caused offense or done something that had a negative impact on the worker's opportunities.

- *Assume responsibility not only for the behavior and attitudes of your work unit but for trying to influence change in your organization.* Although the focus of this book is on the individual manager or supervisor, many decisions affecting the diverse workforce are made at the highest levels of the organization. Such decisions include implementing flextime for women with children or for older workers, granting benefits to life partners of gay and lesbian workers, and, most important, implementing fully the letter and the spirit of the extensive body of law on equal opportunity in the workplace. Managers should seek every opportunity to influence organizational decisions such as these.

- *Finally, understand that it is you, the manager, who ultimately holds the key for releasing the full potential of each person in your work unit.*

Epilogue

There are no easy or pat answers for dealing with the issue of diversity. The managerial responses we have suggested are based on almost twenty years of workplace experience and on the advice of managers who are themselves members of diverse groups. Change is slow and hard, and denial, discomfort, and resistance are ever-present.

But our goal has always been clear: to ensure that managers have basic knowledge of diverse groups from the perspectives of the group members themselves and that a new management voice will emerge that says: "I hear you. I see you as an individual *and* as a member of a group, and I can utilize your differences in a positive way, enhancing both your opportunities and the effectiveness of the workplace!"

Notes

Chapter 3: African-Americans

1. All statistics on population and income are from the following U.S. Bureau of the Census publications: *Demographic State of the Nation: 1990* and *Statistical Abstract of the United States 1992*.
2. Audrey Edwards and Craig Polite, *Children of the Dream* (New York: Doubleday, 1992), pp. 3, 12–13. Cites 1988 U.S. Census Bureau study on net worth as a measure of wealth.

Chapter 4: Asian-Americans

1. U.S. Bureau of the Census, *Statistical Abstract of the United States 1992*.
2. Howard N. Fullerton, "New Labor Force Projections, Spanning 1988 to 2000," *Monthly Labor Review*, November 1989, p. 3.
3. U.S. Bureau of the Census, *Statistical Abstract of the United States 1992*.

Chapter 5: Latinos

1. U.S. Bureau of the Census, *Statistical Abstract of the United States 1992*.
2. Peter Cattan, "The Diversity of Hispanics in the U.S. Workforce," *Monthly Labor Review*, August 1993, p. 3.
3. *New York Times*, April 28, 1993, p. A18, citing Census Bureau data.
4. U.S. Bureau of the Census, *The Hispanic Population in the United States* (March 1991).

Chapter 6: Recent Immigrants

1. Michael J. Mandel and Christopher Farrell, "The New Immigrants: How They're Helping to Revitalize the U.S. Economy," *Business Week*, July 13, 1992, pp. 114, 116.

2. Ibid., p. 114.
3. U.S. Bureau of the Census, *Statistical Abstract of the United States 1992.*
4. Mandel and Farrell, "The New Immigrants," p. 114.
5. Joseph R. Meisenheimer II. "How Do Immigrants Fare in the U.S. Labor Market?" *Monthly Labor Review*, December 1992, pp. 2–19.
6. A *Newsweek* poll reported that 60 percent of Americans think immigration is bad for the country. Reported by Adam Wolfberg, Bob Cohn, and Andrew Murr in "Immigration Backlash," *Newsweek*, August 9, 1993, p. 18; Larry Rohter, "Revisiting Immigration and the Open-Door Policy," *New York Times*, September 19, 1993, News of the Week in Review, p. 4.

Chapter 7: Workers with Disabilities

1. Kevin R. Hopkins and Susan L. Nestleroth, "Willing and Able," *Business Week* (special section in cooperation with the National Organization on Disability), October 28, 1991.
2. President's Committee on Employment of People with Disabilities, *Employer Incentives When Hiring People with Disabilities* (September 1992), p. 9.

Chapter 8: Younger and Older Workers

1. William B. Johnston and Arnold H. Packer, *Workforce 2000: Work and Workers for the 21st Century* (Indianapolis, Ind.: Hudson Institute, 1987), pp. xix, 75–78; Howard N. Fullerton, "New Labor Force Projections, Spanning 1988 to 2000," *Monthly Labor Review*, November 1989, pp. 3–9.
2. Johnston and Packer, *Workforce 2000*, p. 81.
3. American Association of Retired Persons, *Business and Older Workers*, December 1989, p. 3; Catherine D. Fyock, *America's Work Force Is Coming of Age* (Lexington, Mass.: Lexington Books, 1990), p. 2.

Chapter 9: Gays and Lesbians

1. Patrick Rogers, "How Many Gays Are There?" *Newsweek*, February 15, 1993, p. 46.
2. Thomas A. Stewart, "Gay in Corporate America," *Fortune*, December 19, 1991, p. 43.

Chapter 10: Women

1. All statistics on population, positions, and income come from the following: U.S. Department of Labor, *Facts on Working Women* (Octo-

ber 1990), and U.S. Department of Labor, *Working Women: A Chartbook* (August 1991).

2. Ruth Sidel, "Toward a More Caring Society," in Paula Rothenberg, ed., *Race, Class and Gender* (New York: St. Martin's Press, 1992), p. 425.

3. Deborah Swiss and Judith Walker, *Women and the Work Family Dilemma: How Today's Professional Women are Finding Solutions* (New York: John Wiley, 1993).

4. Ronni Sandroff, "Sexual Harassment—The Inside Story," *Working Women*, June 1992, p. 50.

Chapter 11: White Men

1. David Gates, "White Male Paranoia," *Newsweek*, March 29, 1993, p. 49.

Suggested Readings

General

Allport, Gordon. *The Nature of Prejudice*. Reading, Mass.: Addison-Wesley Publishing, 1979.

Crawford, Everett, and Carol J. Romero. *A Changing Nation—Its Changing Labor Force*. National Commission for Employment Policy. Research Report Number 91-04. 1991.

Fernandez, John. *Managing a Diverse Workforce: Regaining the Competitive Edge*. Lexington, Mass.: Lexington Books, 1991.

———. *Racism and Sexism in Corporate Life*. Lexington, Mass.: Lexington Books, 1981.

Gardenswartz, Lee, and Anita Rowe. *Managing Diversity: A Complete Desk Reference and Planning Guide*. Homewood, Ill.: Business One Irwin, 1992.

Glazer, Nathan, and Daniel Moynihan. *Ethnicity: Theory and Experience*. Cambridge, Mass.: Harvard University Press, 1975.

Jackson, Susan E., and Associates. *Diversity in the Workplace: Human Resources Initiatives*. New York: The Guilford Press, 1992.

Jamieson, David, and Julie O'Mara. *Managing Workplace 2000: Gaining the Diversity Advantage*. San Francisco: Jossey-Bass, 1991.

Johnston, William B., and Arnold H. Packer. *Workforce 2000: Work and Workers for the 21st Century*. Indianapolis: Hudson Institute, 1987.

Loden, Marilyn, and Judy Rosener. *Workforce America! Managing Employee Diversity as a Vital Resource*. Homewood, Ill.: Business One Irwin, 1991.

Morrison, Ann M. *The New Leaders: Guidelines on Leadership Diversity in America*. San Francisco: Jossey-Bass, 1992.

Naisbitt, John, and Patricia Aburdene. *Megatrends*. New York: Villard Books, 1990.

Rothenberg, Paula S. *Race, Class and Gender*. New York: St. Martin's Press, 1992.

Simons, George F. *Working Together: How to Become More Effective in a Multicultural Organization.* Los Altos, Calif.: Crisp Publications, 1989.

Thiederman, Sondra. *Bridging Cultural Barriers for Corporate Success: How to Manage the Multicultural Work Force.* Lexington, Mass.: Lexington Books, 1991.

Thomas, R. Roosevelt. *Beyond Race and Gender: Unleashing the Power of Your Total Work Force by Managing Diversity.* New York: AMACOM, 1991.

African-Americans

Davis, George, and Watson Glegg. *Black Life in Corporate America.* Garden City, N.Y.: Doubleday/Anchor Press, 1982.

Dickins, Floyd, Jr., and Jacqueline Dickins. *The Black Manager: Making It in the Corporate World,* rev. ed. New York: AMACOM, 1991.

Edwards, Audrey, and Craig Polite. *Children of the Dream.* New York: Doubleday, 1992.

Hacker, Andrew. *Two Nations: Black and White.* New York: Macmillan, 1992.

Kochman, T. *Black and White Styles in Conflict.* Chicago: University of Chicago Press, 1981.

Terkel, Studs. *Race.* New York: New Press, 1992.

Asian-Americans

Chan, Sucheng. *Asian Americans: An Interpretive History.* Boston: Twayne, 1991.

Kitano, Harry L., and Roger Daniels. *Asian Americans: Emerging Minorities.* Englewood Cliffs, N.J.: Prentice Hall, 1988.

Takaki, Ronald. *Strangers from a Different Shore: A History of Asian Americans.* New York: Penguin Books, 1990.

United States Commission on Civil Rights. *Civil Rights Issues Facing Asian Americans in the 1990's.* February 1992.

Latinos

Brown, Lester B., John Oliver, and J. Jorge Klor de Alva. *Sociocultural and Service Issues in Working with Hispanic American Clients.* Albany: Rockefeller College Press, 1985.

Cattan, Peter. "The Diversity of Hispanics in the U.S. Workforce." *Monthly Labor Review* (August 1993).

De Freitas, Gregory. *Inequality at Work: Hispanics in the U.S. Labor Force.* New York: Oxford University Press, 1991.

Knouse, Stephen B., Paul Rosenfeld, and Amy Culbertson. *Hispanics in the Workplace.* Newbury Park, Calif.: Sage, 1992.

Moore, J., and H. Pachon. *Hispanics in the United States.* Englewood Cliffs, N.J.: Prentice Hall, 1985.

Shorris, Earl. *Latinos.* New York: W. W. Norton, 1992.

Recent Immigrants

Borjas, George. *Friends or Strangers: The Impact of Immigrants in the U.S. Economy.* New York: Basic Books, 1990.

Fierman, Jaclyn. "Is Immigration Hurting the U.S.?" *Fortune* (August 9, 1993).

Kalergis, Mary Morley. *Home of the Brave: Contemporary American Immigrants.* New York: Dutton, 1989.

Mandel, Michael J., and Christopher Farrell. "The New Immigrants: How They're Helping to Revitalize the U.S. Economy." *Business Week* (July 13, 1992).

Meisenheimer, Joseph R., II. "How Do Immigrants Fare in the U.S. Labor Market?" *Monthly Labor Review* (December 1992).

Morganthau, Tom. "America—Still a Melting Pot?" *Newsweek* (August 9, 1993).

Workers with Disabilities

Akabas, Sheila H., Lauren B. Gates, and Donald E. Galvin. *Disability Management.* New York: AMACOM, 1992.

Banta, William F. *AIDS in the Workplace.* New York: Lexington Books, 1993.

Equal Employment Opportunity Commission. *A Technical Assistance Manual on the Employment Provisions of the Americans with Disabilities Act* (January 1992).

Hopkins, Kevin R., and Susan L. Nestleroth. "Willing and Able." *Business Week* (Special Supplement) (October 28, 1991).

New Jersey Division of Developmental Disabilities, Office of Community Education. *Myths and Facts about People with Disabilities* (1992).

President's Committee on Employment of People with Disabilities. *Employer Incentives when Hiring People with Disabilities and Americans with Disabilities Act* (1992).

Younger and Older Workers

American Association of Retired Persons. *Business and Older Workers: Current Perceptions and New Directions for the 1990's* (1989).

Bradford, Lawrence J., and Claire Raines. *Twenty-Something: Managing and Motivating Today's New Work Force.* New York: Master Media, 1991.

Fyock, Catherine D. *America's Work Force Is Coming of Age.* Lexington, Mass.: Lexington Books, 1990.

Maccoby, Michael. *Why Work: Motivating and Leading the New Generation.* New York: Simon and Schuster, 1988.

Massey, Morris. *The People Puzzle.* Reston, Va.: Reston Publishers, 1979.

Mowsesian, Richard. *Golden Goals, Rusted Realities: Work and Aging America.* Far Hills, N.J.: New Horizon Press, 1986.

Shea, Gordon F. *Managing Older Employees.* San Francisco: Jossey-Bass, 1991.

Gays and Lesbians

McNaught, Brian. *Gay Issues in the Workplace.* New York: St. Martin's Press, 1993.

Mickens, Ed. *One Hundred Best Companies for Gay and Lesbian Talent.* New York: Pocket Books, 1994.

———, ed. *Working It Out: The Newsletter for Gay and Lesbian Employment Issues.* New York.

Signorile, Michelangelo. *Queer in America.* New York: Random House, 1993.

Woods, James D. *The Corporate Closet: The Professional Lives of Gay Men in America.* New York: Free Press, 1993.

Women

Aburdene, Patricia, and John Naisbitt. *Megatrends for Women.* New York: Villard Books, 1992.

Ferguson, Trudi, and Joan S. Dunphy. *Answers to the Mommy Track: How Wives and Mothers in Business Reach the Top and Balance Their Lives.* Far Hills, N.J.: New Horizon Press, 1991.

Helegesen, Sally. *The Female Advantage.* New York: Doubleday, 1990.

Loden, Marilyn. *Feminine Leadership or How to Succeed in Business Without Being One of the Boys.* New York: Times Books, 1985.

Swiss, Deborah, and Judith Walker. *Women and the Work Family Dilemma:*

How Today's Professional Women are Finding Solutions. New York: John Wiley, 1993.

White Men

Astrachan, Anthony. *How Men Feel: Their Response to Women's Demands for Equality and Power.* Garden City, N.Y.: Anchor Press/Doubleday, 1986.
Gates, David. "White Male Paranoia." *Newsweek* (March 29, 1993).
Galen, Michele, and Ann Therese Palmer. "White, Male and Worried." *Business Week* (January 31, 1994).
Ross, John Munder. *The Male Paradox.* New York: Simon and Schuster, 1992.
Simons, George F., and G. Deborah Weissman. *Men and Women: Partners at Work.* Los Altos, Calif.: Crisp Publications, 1990.
Tannen, Deborah. *You Just Don't Understand.* New York: Ballantine Books, 1991.

Index